BUILDING STRONG *and* HEALTHY RELATIONSHIPS

BUILDING STRONG *and* HEALTHY RELATIONSHIPS

The Essential Elements for Growing Deeper in Love and Nurturing Strong and Healthy Relationships

DENISE P. LAFORTUNE

iUniverse, Inc.
Bloomington

Building Strong and Healthy Relationships
The Essential Elements for Growing Deeper in Love and Nurturing Strong and Healthy Relationships

iUniverse books may be ordered through booksellers or by contacting:

iUniverse
1663 Liberty Drive
Bloomington, IN 47403
www.iuniverse.com
1-800-Authors (1-800-288-4677)

ISBN: 978-1-4759-2318-6 (sc)
ISBN: 978-1-4759-2319-3 (ebk)

Printed in the United States of America

iUniverse rev. date: 06/04/2012

To my late father, Lucien Paulin, who left behind an imperishable legacy, the Gospel of Jesus Christ, to me. You taught me the best things in life, how to become a vessel of honor that God can use. Thanks, Daddy, for teaching us what really matters in life and for showing us what faith really is. I will be eternally grateful for your example.

* * *

To my mother, Lorca Paulin, for your sacrificial, unconditional love expressed to me on a daily basis. My mom's integrity, humility, love, and compassion for all people have made an indelible impression on my life.

* * *

To my husband, Jean C. Lafortune, whom I've learned a lot from. I'm ready to share a piece of it with the wide world. Our thirteen years of life experience are now becoming live in this book, and people will learn a lot and survive any storms. Love never fails. I will always love you!

CONTENTS

PART 4
How to Let Go of Someone You Love Who Doesn't Treat You Right

PART 5
Missing the Plan of God for Sexuality

PART 6
Building a Strong Family

PART 7
Family Manners for Kids of All Ages

PART 8
Relationship and Friendship Marketplace Open 24/7

ACKNOWLEDGMENTS

I want to extend my personal and sincere thanks to the Holy Spirit. Without your expertise, this project wouldn't have been possible. Thanks for encouraging me to put my heart on paper.

Dr. Jacqueline Narcisse, your godly wisdom and unique insights have made me stronger.

Galilee Ministries Bible College and Seminar Pastoral and Chaplaincy School is the great facilitator. Thanks for bringing us all together and helping us to see the world as our audience.

Reverend Risaldo and First Lady Marie Madeleine Lacombe, I've been blessed to work alongside you. You are the greatest people on the face of the earth. Thanks for believing so passionately in me. Reverend Seaton D. and First Lady Wilson, you have helped me take the message of hope and encouragement to the four corners of the world. To my immediate family, you know me the best, you love me the most, and you have supported me in all my endeavors. I love all of you very much!

PREFACE

Building relationships is of pivotal and fundamental importance in every sphere of life, whether spiritual, social, political, business, family, or ministerial. In her book, *Building Strong and Healthy Relationships,* Minister Lafortune imparts treasures of truths, which are indispensable in building a healthy marriage and family life.

Minister Lafortune shows from her experience and diligent research that building marital and family relationships is not by chance or wishful thinking but by hard work predicated on sound conceptual and pragmatic principles.

It is my privilege and pleasure, based on the facts stated above, to write the preface to this wonderful book. The book is replete with relevant principles and methods that can help to advance and to transform chaotic marital and family relationships. Its ability to guide and steer marriages and family relationships is unquestionable, as evidenced in its content.

I took note of some of the most relevant sections of *Building Strong and Healthy Relationships.* They are as follows:

- How to start a strong relationship. This appears in the introduction of the book. It gives bedrock ideas, beginning with God, on how to begin relationships of different types.
- Charming is deceitfully into wrong relationships.
- The twelve essential ingredients for building a healthy relationship. This aspect of the book lays down twelve basic principles that are prerequisites for a strong relationship from the author's perspective.
- Maintaining a happy relationship. It should be obvious to all that it is not enough to start a relationship; it must also be maintained in an She shows you how to do both.

- Mate selection. I find this insightful, relevant, and interesting, and I am convinced it will be the same for you.
- In addition to the above, she gives guiding light in the areas of sex in marriage, dating, conflict resolution, singleness, sex education, masturbation, preventing pregnancy, how to raise children of destiny, and much more.

The book is also laced with biblical quotations that support her views and provide food for one's soul. She also supplies romantic love quotes that should help to stimulate cold and lukewarm couples to feel the pulsating beat of romantic sentiment in their hearts and bodies and to express it to one another in practical ways. Minister Lafortune comes across in the book as a knowledgeable and persuasive teacher and concludes it as a passionate poet.

Well done, Minister Denise Lafortune. *Building Strong and Healthy Relationships* is destined for success. It is one of the treasured volumes in my library.

Rev. Seaton D. Wilson

Pastor, Speaker, and Author

INTRODUCTION

WHAT MAKES RELATIONSHIPS STRONG AND HEALTHY

Having the thought to write a book about building strong and healthy relationships was not easy, nor my idea or intention. At a period of time, I was in the middle of a crisis where my marriage was falling apart. That's when the Holy Spirit inspired me to write a book about relationships. I knew that if I was confused, others who needed and were looking for a solution to a similar situation were probably confused as well. Sometimes, the way God operates can get you confused if you're in the flesh. See, if I had not experienced the pain and suffering, I would not have been capable of helping others to get the proper solution. "But God hath chosen the foolish things of the world to confound the wise; and God hath chosen the weak things of the world to confound the things which are mighty; and base things of the world, and things which are despised, hath God chosen, yea, and things which are not, to bring to nought things that are: That no flesh should glory in His presence" (1 Cor. 1:27–29). When you need more attention, that's when God will most likely bring hope and comfort to others.

It all started when I was away from home and needed some time to think about what the best thing to do in that particular situation was. As a minister and preacher's wife, I felt I should be a role model. I wanted to respect my vow for better and worse and practice what I preached. It was a very delicate case, and I cannot explain to anyone exactly what that's all about. And it took the wisdom of God to lead me in the right direction. "The fear of the Lord is the beginning of wisdom" (Ps. 11:10). Being in a relationship is not a game. Some people take it lightly, and the result is so painful. There are a lot of divorces and separations, and in certain cases, the children pay the consequences of immature and irresponsible partners. This book will help a lot of people at any age to survive in their relationships, friendships, and partnerships. All those are related in a certain way.

A relationship is defined as a connection with others or sharing with others. There are two kinds of connection: bad connection and good connection. As I go further and deeper into more details about relationships, you will be able to taste the ingredients and the seasonings and spices of the book. We are consecrated kings and queens of the Most High God. In order for us to know how to treat each other, we have to spend time with the King of Kings. We have to see others through God's eyes. We are not to be beaten down or worked over. But we are a precious ointment. We are a royal priesthood. So whoever is in our life should treat us like we are very special. Don't take relationships for granted. Be aware of what you need in a relationship as well as what other people need. This way, your relationship has the best chance of growing and continuing to be strong and healthy. If you are in a situation where a relationship turns sour and someone is hurting and abusing you, it may be best to end or change the relationship. If you are unsure of how to go about this, talk to someone you trust, like a friend, your parents, a counselor, or a youth worker. If you are a Christian and already married, you must recourse to prayer and find yourself a counselor as well before things get worse.

I designed this book to help young people make better choices and make sure they let God help them choose their mate. There is a lot of information as well to equip you to live your best life now while you're waiting for Jesus to come back. There are tools that could help you walk in the road of a strong and healthy relationship. There are certain things you must know before you get engaged in a serious relationship. And the book will help married couples to avoid divorce, which will harm their entire lives. It takes time to heal the wounds of a broken marriage.

PART 1
Starting Point

CHAPTER 1
Starting Point

As with any major building project, it takes a great team to make all the elements come together in a construction. A building cannot stand without a good foundation. You will eventually need a good architect to make the plan, and a team of workers will execute it, along with the materials.

In order to build your strong tower of relationship, friendship, and partnership, you must put God first because He is the designer and builder of the first relationship on the earth. He created a loving garden with all kind of fruits, flowers, and plants, but it was recommended that one of them should not be touched. In any relationship, there is a limit, a line to not cross. And when we do not respect to submit to the laws, there are consequences. The first man did not pay attention to the rules that God Himself established when he first started the relationship. The same thing happens to us. We forget to honor the commitment we have between one another, and when that happens, our actions bring separation, divorce, and conflict. It could be different if we let God design our relationship. All the elements are available to us to build a strong and healthy relationship. The Holy Spirit is there to help us and guide us when we're making a decision. It is so beautiful when two people can combine together in the garden of love, respect, and trust. You will be able to stand against all evils. "Healthy relationship need to watery in the source of the fruit of the Spirit: Love, joy, peace, longsuffering, gentleness, goodness, meekness, temperance, faithfulness" (Gal. 5:22–23). If we live in the Spirit, let us also walk in the Spirit.

CHAPTER 2

How to Start a Relationship

Are you having trouble finding someone who is just right for you? Do you want to get closer to someone? Here are some steps to follow:

1. Let God be the center of your relationship.
2. Don't go by the appearance. Someone can be awesome at anything and be smart, funny, and much more. It could be all demonstrations, and you will find yourself so disappointed and will regret the day you met that person. Don't go by the look. Your judgment could be wrong. Try to find some good values.
3. Look for someone you can easily talk to. The most important part of any relationship is communication. If you cannot communicate effectively with your partner, your relationship will probably not go far.
4. Talk to and befriend the person you think is special. Most people don't like to jump straight into a relationship, especially girls. Find a reason to talk to the person. Make sure he or she wants to talk to you. Just talk about something that keeps the conversation going.
5. Be yourself. Don't lie just to get a special person's heart. If he or she finds out later and you're in the middle of a deep relationship or maybe a time when you really need that person, he or she will leave you for good.
6. Be yourself at all times. Try not to show off much, or you could embarrass yourself.
7. Take things slowly. Don't be too needy. He or she will think you're just an annoying friend, and you probably don't want him or her to think that. If you give it some time, things could work out. Once you have established first contact, remember not to squeeze the person. Try to continue doing a normal routine, with him or her in mind, rather than changing your whole life around him or her. Hopefully, he or she will want to have a relationship with you.

TIPS

- Try to look nice. Looks count for first impressions.
- Make conversations more meaningful. If a girl thinks you are talking to her only because you want to get with her, she will not be too interested.
- Be sure to maintain eye contact when possible. This is especially so when talking about things you have in common. Allow eye contact to linger even into silences. If your mark allows this eye contact to linger as well, it's a good sign. If the lingering eye contact begins to feel awkward, just smile.
- If you've known this person for a very long time, remind him or her of good times. He or she will love reliving memories. For example, you're in seventh grade. You've known the girl you like since third grade. Remind her of really good times you had—for example, funny things that happened to both of you, someone you both know, bad substitute teachers you've had, and on and on. It just makes her want to talk to you more!
- Try to be close with the person's family. It will strengthen the relationship.

WARNINGS

- Never compromise your morals. If the person you are interested in is not interested in you, then move on. Some people are very polite and don't realize immediately the other person isn't interested. But, given time, it should become apparent. In the meantime, take it slow. This person can abuse your attraction to his or her benefit.
- If you feel like you need time to decide, do not hesitate to take it. Your goal is to find a good mate for a relationship. If someone feels wrong, think things through twice before acting.
- To really get a good relationship, do not get involved in sexual intimacy. Many people have started out hot and heavy, but it usually burns out fast. This section in the garden should not be touched until the day of your blessing. That is why so many hearts are broken. They ate the fruit in the middle of garden before they became "one flesh," as the minister pronounced.

CHAPTER 3
Stop the Bleeding

So many people have failed in their relationship for lack of the knowledge of things they should or should not do. Healthy relationships do not start in a bed or chasing after someone. Especially for the girls, they could abuse your attraction to their benefit. Everybody is looking for love, but be careful how and where you're searching for the one you want to spend your life with. The Bible gives some instructions on how to find your partner:

1. Let God choose the one who is best for you and well deserves someone like you, the one who will be there for you in the good and bad times and the one who will love you for who you are. The Bible says, "Love overlooks a person's faults." God proves to us what true love is. "For God so loved the world that He gave His only begotten son, that whosoever believeth in Him should not perish but have everlasting life" (John 3:16). Where there is true love, there is sacrifice. The new generation needs to know they could have a good relationship without having sex. True love will wait. That's not always easy, but love believes the best in every person. We could stop the bleeding of the hurting heart when practicing the real principle of a true relationship.
2. Recognize the importance of respect in a relationship. Sometimes you tend to go over the limits if you see the person is genuinely interested in you and you think that you've already won the person's heart or that the friendship is stable by now. Big mistake! You should respect one another. Ultimately, that will make the bones of your relationship a lot stronger and healthier.
3. Let trust be the solid rock on which that relationship is standing. It's a cancer in the bones when you don't trust someone. It is impossible to have a strong relationship without trust. Don't ever get involved

with someone you cannot trust. You will never be happy. You'll be so miserable that you will wish you'd never met that person. Don't lie to one another. Be truthful. If ever you have to lose someone because you're telling the truth, it was not meant to be. Wait for the right one. He or she will always like to hear the truth, even when it could be hurtful. That's the truth, nothing to be regretted when you know you are right and the truth will set you free. Any relationship built on lies will destroy. There is nothing real. You cannot produce any good fruit. It's totally a disaster.

Charming Is Deceitful

Beauty is vain, but a woman or man who fears the Lord shall be praised. The fear of God is the beginning of wisdom. Don't ever choose a man or woman by his or her beauty. Be wise enough, especially in these days. Apparently, the beauty is to die for, and you could not resist the charm. Don't fall in love with what you see on the outside. It could be so deceitful. Take time to look for some good qualities that will make you live happily ever after. Who can find a virtuous woman? Who can find a good man? Through the Bible, we find some good examples, some role models, and we could apply these in our lives as well today. There are human beings just like you in the Bible. If they could make a difference and leave a legacy, why can't you?

Daniel was a teenager when he was brought to Babylon, but he purposed in his heart that he would not defile himself with the portion of the king's meat, nor with the wine that he drank. Therefore, he requested of the prince of the eunuchs that he might not defile himself (Dan. 1:8). When God sees your heart and your willingness to make a difference in your relationship, He will bring favor and tender love. The desire of your heart will be fulfilled, and you will have exactly what you are looking for, the everlasting love.

Esther was one of a kind. She was not born in the country that she became the queen of. About all the other young ladies who were there, why, they could satisfy the king's desire. All the others were so beautiful as well, but the difference was that Esther already carried the King of Kings inside of her heart. All the other kings should bow down.

When you observe all the principles of God, there is no limit for you. The impossible could be possible, and God will bless you exceedingly abundant, above and beyond your imagination if you keep your relationship pure, exempt of sin. Do not forget you are representing the kingdom of the Most High. You must know the protocol of the kingdom. Esther submitted herself to the protocol of palace preparation for one reason. The only way to be transformed and conformed into an acceptable bride for the king was to submit to the protocols of the palace, soaking in the oil!

What to Conquer

We in the body of Christ experience transformation when the anointing of God descends upon us. Understood like this, I would have to say the anointing is for Him, not us! The oil is on us, but it is for Him! Money, fame, and fear can motivate people to do some crazy things. They also share a sad legacy with another people. Others will sacrifice their reputation and every ounce of their self-esteem for one minute in the national spotlight or a few moments of stolen pleasures in another person's bed. Whatever impresses you attracts you. Whatever you pursue becomes your purpose. What are you pursuing, the king or the kingdom? It stands to reason that most of the young maidens ushered into this ancient world's most important beauty contest would be enamored with the king's palace. Most people would find it hard to blame them. Today, far too many Christians are enamored with finite finery and earthly benefits of God's kingdom rather than its king. The anointed one always makes a difference.

CHAPTER 4

The Twelve Essential Ingredients for Building a Healthy Relationship

You can use reliable tools, many of which have not been taught in our culture, to create a strong and healthy relationship. If you want to have a really strong and healthy relationship, follow these simple guidelines:

- **Do not expect anyone to be responsible for your happiness.** Accept yourself. Respect yourself. Love yourself. Take good care of yourself. If you want, you can always find something to do that makes you feel good about yourself right now. Love yourself, so pursue your true needs. Light up your true desires. Too often, relationships fail because someone is unhappy and blames his or her partner for making him or her that way. Your life is only under your control. Keep reminding yourself you are good enough to have a happy life and healthy relationship. Make yourself happy, and then share with one another.
- **Make and keep clear agreements.** Respect the differences between yourself and your partner. Don't expect him or her to agree with you on everything. Reach a mutual agreement or plan, and then commit to it. Leave the partner if you can't reach any agreement or you find he or she always makes excuses for breaking the agreement or plan. If you say you're going to meet your partner for lunch at noon, be on time, or call if you're going to be late. If you agree to have a monogamous relationship, keep that agreement and/or tell the truth about any feelings you're having about someone else before you act on them. Keeping agreements shows respect for yourself and your partner, as well as creating a sense of trust and safety.

- **Use communication to establish a common ground to understand different points of view and to create a mutual, collaborative agreement or plan.** You can either choose to be right, or you can have a successful relationship. You can't always have both. Most people argue to be right about something. They say, "If you loved me, you would . . ." and argue to hear the other say, "Okay, you're right." If you are generally more interested in being right, this approach will not create a healthy relationship. Having a strong and healthy relationship means that you have your experience and your partner has his or hers. You learn to love, share, and learn from experiences. If you can't reach any mutual agreement, that doesn't mean either of you is wrong or bad. It only means you suit each other.
- **Approach your relationship as a learning experience.** Each one has important information for you to learn. For example, do you often feel bossed around in your relationship, or do you feel powerless? When a relationship is not working, we usually feel something familiar. We are attracted to the partner with whom we can learn the most, and sometimes the lesson is to let go of a relationship that no longer serves us. A truly healthy relationship will consist of both partners who are interested in learning and expanding a relationship so it continues to improve.
- **Tell the unarguable truth.** If you want true love, be truthful to yourself and your partner. Many people are taught to lie to protect someone's feelings, either their own or the partner's. Lies create disconnection between you and your relationship, even if your partner never finds out about it. The unarguable truth is about your true feelings. Your partner can argue about anything that happens outside of you, but he or she cannot rationally deny your feelings. Here are some examples:
    - "I felt scared when I saw you talking to him at the party."
    - "I feel angry when you hang up on me."
    - "I felt sad when you walked out during our fight and didn't want to be around me."
- **Do not do anything for your partner if it comes with an expectation of reciprocation.** The things you do for your partner must always be done because you chose to do them and you wanted to do them. Do not hold your good deeds over his or her head at a later time. Keeping score in a relationship will never work. A person is less likely to notice and value all contributions of his or her partner as much as his or her own.

- **Forgive one another.** Forgiveness is a decision of letting go of the past and focusing on the present. It's about taking control of your current situation. Talk about the issue. Try to reach a mutual agreement on how to handle the situation in the future, and then commit to it. If you can't reach an agreement, it's a bad sign. If you learn from the past and do not repeat the same pattern, it's a good sign. It's the only way to prevent yourself from more disappointment, anger, or resentment. Respect your partner. When your partner tells you to leave him or her alone, do give the time and space.
- **Review your expectations.** Try to be as clear as you can about any expectations, including acceptable and unacceptable behavior and attitudes, especially toward money. Make sure you don't expect your partner to fulfill every need in your life. One person cannot be everything to you. Everybody needs love, intimacy, affection, and affirmation, but your partner cannot alone give you all of that. You need to get some from your friends and family, but first and foremost, love yourself. Attempting to change someone else's mode of processing or personality style won't work and will create derailments.
- **Be responsible.** Here's a new definition: Responsible means you have the ability to respond. Respond to real problems and your true needs. It does not mean you are to blame. There is tremendous power in claiming your creation. If you've been snippy to your partner, own up to it, and get serious about why you are jealous and how you might do it differently next time. If you are unhappy in your relationship, get curious about why this situation seems similar to others from your past and how you might create a better relationship for yourself rather than dwell in anger or resentment or try to change your partner instead.
- **Appreciate yourself and your partner.** In the midst of an argument, it can be difficult to find something to appreciate. Start by generating appreciation in moments of nonstress. That way, when you need to be able to do it during a stressful conversation, it will be easier. One definition of appreciation is to be sensitively aware so you don't have to be sugarcoating anything. So tell your beloved that you appreciate him or her and you don't want to argue but to talk and make it better.
- **Admit your mistakes and say you're sorry.** Right after a misunderstanding or argument, tell your partner to give you some

time to think of the wrong and right things that you and he or she did. Tell your partner to do the same thing, and talk to him or her after ten to fifteen minutes. Tell your partner to give you time to talk, and explain why you were angry, the wrong things you did, the things he or she did that you did not like, and what you would like him or her to change. Ask your partner to do the same thing, and give him or her a fair chance to talk and explain as well. This will make your relationship stronger and help strengthen the communication between you and your partner.

- **Spend some quality time together.** No matter how busy you two are, there is always an excitement when you do something together, when you share your precious time. Play a sport, eat at a restaurant, or watch your favorite movies together. You will feel the magic of love and connection that you have with each other.

The Key of Success

- Know yourself, be honest with yourself, and love yourself first! Only then can you truly appreciate and love someone else.
- Take good care of yourself. Treating yourself with respect and love is as important as respecting and loving your partner. Conduct yourself with dignity, even if you're very familiar with one another.
- Recognize that all good relationships are based upon mutual respect. If you do not feel respect for your partner or believe your partner is losing respect for you, then consider ways of rebuilding it immediately. Respect is the key. If you have true respect for one another, then nothing can go wrong. You just have to find the right person to respect. This is the hard part.
- Ask questions, clarify, and don't assume. Do not talk if your mind is not clear or full of anger. When you feel hurt, do not say, "You don't love me," "You never loved me," "Let's break up," or "When do you want to break up?" You will regret it one day. Tell him or her that you feel hurt and ask for clarification first.

- Treat your partner the way you want to be treated. Be gentle and kind. Apologize if your partner feels hurt. Apology does not mean you are bad. It only means you care. When anger fills you, it will surely burst out of your mouth if you open it. Calm down first, think it through, and then try to talk. When your partner asks to be left alone, do not blame or criticize. Show your respect and support by giving him or her the time and space to calm down and think it through first. But do not leave any unresolved problem for too long.

- Be the first to tell your partner, either positive or negative. Trust is as essential as respect. If you want your partner to trust you, trust him or her first. Letting your partner play guessing games may lead to misunderstanding and frustration. But don't just tell him or her the issue. Also talk about your plan to resolve it.
- Strike while the iron is cold. Know when to be reflective and invoke principles. When the house is burning is no time to teach fire safety principles.
- Communicate with your partner. Without communication, there is no relationship. Stay in touch by, for example, calling your partner, even if it's just to say "hi" and "I love you."
- Avoid any activity that could cause your partner to experience doubt, suspicion, or distrust. Build your credibility, and earn trust and respect by always communicating truthfully and proactively. And always keep your word. In this way, if something happens that looks incriminating, your partner will believe you if you claim you are innocent. Past behavior predicts future actions. Building a solid foundation of trust and integrity will take you far. However, ultimately your life and where it takes you is more important than your obligations to someone else. If there is trust in a relationship, you should be able to do what you want. You aren't responsible for making someone else jealous.
- Always make sure to show your partner that you appreciate him or her. Whether it's calling to check in, saying "I love you," or just spending your Saturday night together, the possibilities are endless.
- Know when to say no, and know when time and space are actually constructive tools.
- Recognize that it is not always a good idea to answer certain questions with absolute truth if they bring emotional harm. "Do you sometimes think about your ex?" and "Do I look fat in these pants?" are both loaded questions. In a relationship, answer questions honestly but with tact and grace. For example, you could say, "I think you have other pants that look better on you" instead of "They don't" or "They do."
- Remember that what you don't do is as important as what you do.

- Avoid flirting with others, especially previous partners or coworkers. Doing so may spur romantic feelings for another. There is nothing wrong with being friends with someone you are attracted to. Just keep flirting out of the friendship.
- Tell your partner how you really feel about your ex and why you're no longer romantically involved. Don't ever lie or cheat on your partner. However, one of those questions it's best not to answer totally honestly is this: "Do you still think about your ex?" If you have fond memories, don't dwell on them, and assure your partner that, while you occasionally remember places you went or things that happened, you are so much happier to be with your present partner. Period. Don't launch into a rehashing of the old days with the ex. Or don't talk at length about the good times you had together or things you did together.
- Know that it can help to learn the difference between healthy and unhealthy relationships. That way, you can see potential problems and recognize when they arise. (Remember, it's likely you would see something unhealthy at some point, so don't be alarmed or shocked, as there is no perfect relationship because we are all human and fallible.) If you see something unhealthy in your relationship, try to work out why this is, and see if you can work toward resolving it.

PART 2

Be on Safe Ground

CHAPTER 5
Be on Safe Ground

Keep your expectations about the relationship realistic. Marriage should not be on your mind if you've been talking for a week, for example. Nor should you think that relationship will solve your problems or you'll never be alone again or anything like that. Relationships can be wonderful things, but be realistic about them. Just as one can feel lonely in a crowd, one can also feel lonely occasionally when in a relationship. That doesn't mean the relationship is bad. It only means you're feeling a little down. Don't ascribe too much importance to it unless these feelings linger and begin to dominate your days and nights. If this happens, seek help. You may be spiraling into a depression.

Do not assume that any one relationship will be perfect. It is human to experience disagreements and emotional pain. Working past these issues may be an ongoing struggle. Do not call it quits when you do argue. When in a state of anger, we cannot rationalize and often find ourselves losing control by saying things we don't mean. Hang in there, and try to work it out before finalizing a breakup that you will regret afterward. That said, if you find you are arguing more and more, examine the possible reasons, and talk it over together. There is no such thing as a perfect relationship. Sure, you'll be compromising most of the time. But don't get shocked or overly depressed because of arguments or fights. This will come for sure. Without arguments and fights, your relationship will not grow stronger.

CHAPTER 6

How to Bring Love into a Relationship

When a building is being constructed, groundwork is critically important. If the foundation is faulty, the whole building will be unstable. If the foundation is solid, the building will be stable and stand firm under stress.

The same is true when building loving relationships. We need to have a solid foundation on which to build. If we don't, the whole structure of the relationship is in danger. If we have a solid base of love, we can experience deep and meaningful relationships.

Although all of us desire to be genuinely loving, we all have different natural capacities for receiving and expressing love. Our capacity to love is also based on how we have responded to things that life has thrown at us. Life is a mixed bag. Some people encounter obstacles and difficulties and become increasingly bitter and hard-hearted over the years. Others tend to become more open, kind, and gentle over time. The majority of us are somewhere in the middle.

If you are in a relationship, it can be difficult to know how to let it progress. This should help:

1. Be willing to let love in your relationship and give love back 100 percent.
2. Don't rush into saying, "I love you." Take the time to realize what you're saying—that is, wait until it means something. Unless you can

feel like this is a promise—that is, you will feel like this for the rest of your life—then don't say it!

3. Make sure you trust, admire, and respect the person you are with. Can you see being with him or her forever? Can you really talk to each other? Can you be honest with and support each other? Do you have meaningful conversations? Do you mean something to each other? Is the relationship exclusive, serious, long term, mature, meaningful, loving, trustful, respectful, and so on? If the answer is yes, then you may be heading toward love.
4. Take the physical aspect of the relationship slowly as well. This will give you time to develop other aspects of your relationship, like the verbal, psychological, mental, emotional, affectionate, and other kinds of intimacy/closeness that has nothing to do with the physical stuff.
5. Don't let your life completely revolve around him or her. Your partner will find that you have other priorities. It's a sign of self-respect.

Helpful Ideas

- When you are comfortable with that person, open up, and let him or her in your life.
- Trust your instincts.
- Make time for each other.
- Spend time apart as well.
- Connect/bond on a deeper level (more than sex and so forth) with one another.
- Let there be time for the emotional, psychological, mental, verbal, and so forth intimacy or closeness to grow, expand, and develop (and so on).

Maintaining a Happy Relationship

A relationship can be a great way to have fun and create a special friendship as well as learn a lot about yourself and others. You might have a sense that a relationship is happy and going well when you can laugh and enjoy someone's company. Each of you provides safety and support. Each of you shares ideas and feelings. Each of you respects the other. Every relationship is unique, and you may have your own way of knowing that a relationship is going well. But it is important that you still put effort into it.

Suggestions for Keeping Relationships Strong

- **Trust and be honest.** Learning to trust and be honest with someone may take time. It can also be an important ingredient in a healthy relationship. As you spend more time with someone and start to share experiences together, your level of trust may increase.
- **Keep communicating.** It is a good idea to keep the lines of communication open about what is happening in your life and how you feel about it. When people share their opinions and feelings, they develop a greater understanding of each other's likes and dislikes. It may also help to work out what each other wants from the relationship. Talking about some things may be hard, particularly if you are sad or angry about something with someone. It gives you lots of new things to share. This may also help your relationships continue to grow and be fun and interesting.
- **Spend time with yourself.** Spending time with yourself can be fun. It can also help you understand yourself and your relationship with others. If possible, spend time getting to know yourself. This may feel a bit scary at first, but over time, it can become less weird and more enjoyable. You may want to start by doing something you really enjoy. You can spend time with yourself doing lots of things like being active, listening to music, or reading. Being by yourself does not mean you are alone. You are with yourself. You may want to think about what and where you want to go in life and whom you might want to take with you.
- **Manage arguments or differences of opinions.** People naturally sometimes have differences of opinions. When we disagree with each other, we may feel angry or frustrated. Not letting someone know your opinion, not having your opinion heard, or having to accept someone's opinion without discussion may add to your frustrations and make a relationship difficult. It is a good idea to express your opinions. Let the other person know you are listening to him or her, and try to reach an understanding between the two of you. You might choose to respect his or her right to an opinion but not accept his or her opinions, agree to disagree, see the other person's point of view, or accept that your opinion needs to change. It may be helpful to write it down as a way of expressing yourself.

- **Try to be accepting of difference.** It is uncommon to care about someone who has different ideas, interests, and opinions to your own. Sometimes it can be difficult managing differences. It may be helpful to calmly discuss those differences, or it may also be appropriate to agree to disagree. Respecting someone else's choices and opinions may help him or her to respect yours. It may be good to remember that we are all different and the world could be really boring if we were all the same. Trying to accept differences, especially between the people we like and ourselves, can help make you and your relationship healthier and stronger.
- **Respect each other's space.** Hanging out together is important in getting to know each other, and it can also be great fun. Giving each other space from time to time is also important. Enjoying the company of a number of people, like your friends (and not just the person who you are having a relationship with), may help you to expand your interests.

Recognize the Signs of a Bad Relationship

While a good relationship is the source of joy and fulfillment, a bad one can be the cause of fear, unhappiness, and, in some cases, violence. No relationship is without flaws. However, a bad or unhealthy one leaves those in it with scars. Learn to recognize the signs of a bad relationship, and then pursue for the best solution.

Red Flags

- **Compare your past lifestyle to your present.** If you have hobbies or interests you once enjoyed but no longer pursue, consider why. If you feel pressure from your partner to end these activities, it is a cause for concern.
- **Consider your relationship with others.** If you display a general lack of respect for the relationships you have with family and friends or seek to interfere with them, it could be a sign of a bad relationship.
- **Write down any comments and gestures your mate makes toward your appearance.** When a mate vocalizes your insecurities by ridiculing your dress or physical appearance or has pressured you to

change this physical appearance in some way, then your relationship might be unhealthy.

- **Think about the way you settle disputes.** If you experience fear, yelling, put-downs, or physical violence, your relationship is unhealthy.
- **Notice other signs of control.** This includes unequal control of resources like food, money, and transportation or being obligated or pressured to have sex.

A relationship that exhibits one or two signs of unhealthiness is not necessarily cause for abandonment. In relationships such as this, it is important to zero in on the area of concern and address it effectively. For those who find disagreements with their partners are settled by yelling or hashing out unfairly, couples counseling could be the answer.

PART 3

Singleness

CHAPTER 7
Singleness

Adam was the first person to experience singleness, but this didn't last long. God declared that it was "not good for the man to be alone. I will make a companion who will help him." The result was creation of the woman, and Adam became the first married man. Clearly, marriage was God's intention for the human race. He expected that a man and woman would unite together for companionship, sexual fulfillment, perpetuation of the human race, and partnership in their use and control of the environment.

Even at the beginning, surely God knew that a happy, blissful marriage would not be everyone's experience. The tendency for men to die earlier than women and the influence of wars that often reduce the male population both would ensure that there never would be enough men for all the women in the world. Further, in this imperfect and sinful world, there are those who fear intimacy with the opposite sex, find it difficult to make commitments, have marriages that break up, or never enter a heterosexual marriage in the first place because of their homosexuality. In addition, some people lose their spouses in death, and for a variety of reasons, others choose not to marry.

These people are not necessarily unhealthy or unnatural because they are single. Some people, for example, prefer to remain single because they have no desire to marry. Others choose to remain single so they can devote themselves more fully to God's work. For many believers, the single state is a special gift that God bestows on select people, including some who are not at all enthusiastic about being recipients of the gift.

Paul elaborated on this in detail in 1 Corinthians 7, where he discussed sex and presented a high view of marriage but also considered singleness. Marriage and singleness are both gifts from God, we are told. Noting that he himself was unmarried, the apostle wrote very positively about the single lifestyle. Marriage is fine, he said, but singleness is even better.

I am trying to spare you the extra problems that come with marriage. An unmarried man can spend his time doing the Lord's work and thinking about how to please Him. But a married man can't do that so well. He has to think about his earthly responsibilities and how to please his wife. His interests are divided. In the same way a woman who is no longer married or has never been married can be more devoted to the Lord in body and in spirit, a married woman must be concerned about her earthly responsibilities and how to please her husband. I am saying this for your benefit, not to place restrictions on you. I want you to do whatever will help you to serve the Lord best with as few distractions as possible.

Here, Paul elevates the single life as a way of living in which the individual can give undivided devotion to Christ, free of the greater responsibilities and financial pressures that often come with marriage. But how many Christian singles, even deeply committed believers, really view life like this? Maybe it was fine for Paul and some super-spiritual single people today to view their unmarried state as a way to "serve the Lord best with as few distractions as possible." It seems more likely, however, that many single believers put greater emphasis on wondering why they have not found a life partner, struggling at times to fit into society, praying and looking for a mate, grappling with feelings of inadequacy, or resisting pressures from parents who are critical of their unmarried adult children. Others may be active in building their lives and careers apart from having a mate. These people are not flying aimlessly, going in circles until they are able to land into a marriage. They have decided to move on with their lives, but even for them, singleness is not easy. For many, unmarried life brings a number of problems.

CHAPTER 8
The Causes of Singleness Problems

What is there about singleness that can lead to problems? To answer, let us look at five major groups of single people. Each has a somewhat unique set of challenges and needs relating to their being unmarried.

1. **Some have not yet found a mate or have decided to postpone marriage temporarily.** It is well known that, in recent years, there has been a growing trend for people to postpone marriage. In the latest US Census, for example, the median age for marriage had increased from 23.2 to 26.7 years for men and from 20.8 to 25 years for women, compared to the previous generation. Many younger people want to travel, get established in their careers, or otherwise experience the freedoms of adulthood before taking on the responsibilities of marriage. Unlike their parents when they were getting started, many singles today conclude that getting married later is preferable because it gives them more time to decide what they want in their lives and in a spouse. In addition, changing social attitudes have led many, including Christians, to conclude that sex apart from marriage is natural and acceptable, so there is no need to get married before engaging in sexual intercourse. The apostle Paul wrote that people who cannot control themselves should give in to their urges and have sexual intercourse outside of marriage. In time, many of these people will marry, but often they have little motivation to hasten the process until the right one comes along. Students, individuals whose work involves travel, those getting started in the business world or preparing for a professional career, and many others have every intention of getting married, but they have no problem with waiting a few years. These singles face many of the

problems and challenges that concern all unmarried people, but there is no rush to find a mate. There is no panic over prospects of being single and no assumption that life is on hold until they get married. These people have chosen to postpone marriage and perhaps even kiss dating good-bye for a while. They have a healthy outlook, and they are not often seen in counselors' offices with a concern about still being single. For them, singleness is not seen as a tragedy that has come as the result of unwanted circumstances. Instead, singleness is viewed as a choice that can be changed later. Others are unmarried and more concerned about singleness. They live with a waiting mentality that says, "I can't make any plans on my own, and I shouldn't make any major decisions because these might have to change if I get married to somebody whose ideas and goals are different." Well-meaning advice may reinforce such an attitude, but sometimes insensitive friends or relatives imply that life isn't complete until one has a mate. This is an attitude that can immobilize single people so they are always looking for the appearance of a possible mate, living in the future and waiting for that time when marriage will make life complete. For these people, every date is seen as a potential opportunity for marriage. Their dating partners sense this and back away quickly. This eager attitude also leads some people to jump at the first opportunity for marriage and discover later that they have landed in marital chaos. "I would rather be single and wish I was married," said one of my friends, "than to be married and wish I were still single."

2. **Some choose to stay single.** Early in life, some people make the deliberate decision to remain single, but for others, this decision is more of a gradual awareness and acceptance of the fact that marriage is unlikely. Of course, there are good reasons for choosing to remain single. These include a conviction that singleness is God's calling, a shortage of eligible marriage partners, a desire for continuing freedom, or belief that commitment to a marriage is impractical. Others may conclude that singleness is preferable because they have had experiences with marriage or watched their friends go through painful divorces. They may be committed to careers that demand long hours and the freedom to move. They may feel shy and self-conscious with the opposite sex. Or they fear intimacy. Regardless of the reasons, increasing numbers of people appear to be content to stay single, and in many countries, this is becoming more acceptable for both men and women.

3. **Some have had marriages break up.** If a marriage has been unhappy for a long time, its ending may bring at least a temporary sense of relief. Even so, to be single again following a separation or divorce is not easy. Many experience loneliness, struggles in adjusting to the transition from marriage back to singleness, and feelings of failure along with bitterness. Often, the person experiences difficulties with self-image as the formerly married person struggles with questions such as, "Where do I fit now?" or "Who am I?" Criticism or social ostracism that comes from others, including family members, friends, unforgiving church members, or insensitive coworkers, can make all of this worse. People who have lost a mate through death usually feel the sympathy and support of friends or relatives, but this kind of compassionate caring rarely comes to those whose marriages have ended through separation or divorce.
4. **Some have lost a mate.** Grief, pain, loneliness, and great sense of loss comes to those who have lost a mate. Perhaps only those who have had similar experiences really can understand. As we have seen, when a death occurs, relatives and friends reach out to offer support and comfort, but the grief persists long after the funeral is over and the friends have gone back to their regular routines. The loneliness does not leave. There is continuing sadness, emptiness, and the pressures of learning to live alone, making decisions that previously were shared and thinking of oneself as single again. All of this may be especially difficult for those who are older.
5. **Some have other reasons for singleness.** Overlapping with the above categories are situations that reduce the likelihood of marriage. These include:
   a. Chronic illness and disabilities, both physical and mental, that reduce the person's potential for marriage and could interfere with the development of a fulfilling relationship with someone of the opposite sex.
   b Unrealistic views about what members of the opposite sex are like.
   c Immaturity, including an inability to give and an unwillingness to accept responsibility or to make commitments.
   d A belief that cohabitation is better than marriage, despite the accumulation of evidence showing that cohabitation can have a number of traps and adverse effects on subsequent marriage.

CHAPTER 9
Preventing Problems of Singleness

Following a conference for singles, one of the participants wrote a note to the speaker. "Single or married, we all live in the same world. We are all part of a family, whether present or removed, and shouldn't we have common interests and concerns? Singles as well as married couples can be very narrow in their perspectives, all wrapped up in their own concerns and with little interest in the world around them. The single person should have a greater incentive to aggressively reach out and take part in all of life. We singles tend to be too timid! Whether you are married or single is incidental. The point is that you can control the quality of your life. For the Christian, this should have special meaning."

Somebody has suggested that it's a terrible waste of a life to never accept one's singleness, to resent it, and to spend life waiting for somebody to come along. Many people don't like being single and wish things were different. Nothing is wrong with this attitude. But a lot of these same people jump into their careers, live life to the fullest, build friendships, and sometimes have significant ministries without waiting for somebody else to fulfill them.

CHANGING UNHEALTHY ATTITUDES TOWARD SINGLES

Something is wrong with a church that sees single adults as misfits, has no place in the body for unmarried people, lacks programs to meet the needs of singles, and shows no understanding (or desire to understand) their struggles, especially if the single person is divorced.

Pastors and other leaders can set the tone for changing unhealthy attitudes toward singles. Married persons can be encouraged to welcome singles into the church and into their homes. It may be helpful to remind people that Paul was single. He might not be welcome in some churches today, and certainly he would be unacceptable to many pulpit committees who maintain a prejudice against single pastors.

Stimulate Ministries to Singles

While single adults should be integrated into the mainstream of the church, there also can be programs to meet their unique needs. Singles groups in the church (or groups combining singles from several smaller churches) are most helpful when they

- reach out to newcomers;
- avoid an emphasis on matchmaking or dating;
- provide for and, at times, involve the children of singles in social gatherings;
- are sensitive to the personal and spiritual needs of group members;
- are led by mature, sensitive, preferably unmarried leaders.

Don't forget that singles have different needs and interests. An eighty-seven-year-old widow and a twenty-two-year-old college student are both single, but the similarity stops about there. They mostly have different needs, perspectives, and hopes. Because most churches are small, it is not easy or even wise to have programs for everybody. Still, Christians need to think creatively about ways to minister to one another, including singles, whether or not we have detailed programs for everybody. When there are teaching, worship, social interaction, and opportunities for service, many singles are willing to come together. Often, this kind of interaction and outreach has potential for preventing many singles' problems and providing ways for handling existing problems before they get worse.

The Bible and Mate Selection

The Bible makes many positive statements about marriage, but it says little about mate selection. Jesus gave his sanction to marriage, and so did Paul, but neither discussed how marriage partners should be chosen.

This silence may reflect the fact that, in biblical times, choosing a mate was not a responsibility for the couple as it is for many people today. Consider, for example, the choice of a wife for Isaac. His father sent a servant on a long journey to find a suitable candidate. The servant sought divine guidance in this process, and God gave a sign from heaven that Rebekah was the right one. Her parents were consulted, and they asked the girl if she was willing to leave her family (perhaps forever) and travel to marry a man she had never met. Nobody ever talked about love or dating. Everybody assumed that the Lord was guiding in this choice, but personality, compatibility, sexual attraction, love, or the bride and groom's preferences were not part of the decision-making process. With Jacob, the situation was different. He was away from his parents when he fell in love, so the groom went directly to Rachel's father, although not to the bride.

Both Isaac and Jacob married later in life, but apparently many people in biblical times married young, sometimes as early as age twelve or thirteen. The parents usually made the decision, just as they still do in parts of the world today, but the young person could make his or her wishes known and sometimes even refused to go along with the parental choice. After a marriage had been arranged, there often was a period of unbreakable betrothal or engagement, followed by a ceremony of marriage. Unlike Mary and Joseph, who were in this engagement stage when Mary became pregnant, it appears that sometimes the groom didn't even see the bride's face until they were in bed together after the wedding. Even the thought of such a prospect can send shivers of anxiety up and down the spines of many contemporary single people, no doubt including some who might be reading these words.

- **Do we have biblical guidelines for choosing a mate today?** Perhaps there really is only one: believers are to marry only other believers. Christians should not marry non-Christians. "Don't team with those who are unbelievers. How can goodness be a partner with wickedness? How can light live with darkness?" we read in Paul's second letter to the Corinthians. "How can believers partner with unbelievers?" This is a union of harmony either as business partners or marriage partners. A similar idea is emphasized in 1 Corinthians and specifically applied to marriage when Paul states that the unmarried woman is free to marry whomever she wishes but only if the marriage is acceptable to the Lord, which would imply that she must marry a fellow believer.

- **What about divine guidance?** Just as Abraham's servant expected and experienced divine leading in selecting a wife for Isaac, perhaps most Christians would agree that we still can expect God's leading in mate selection. Several biblical passages teach that believers can expect divine leading, even though this may not come in dramatic or seemingly miraculous ways. Christians are divided over the issue of whether God has only one choice for a person who is seeking a life partner. It is difficult to find biblical support for the idea that, in all of the universe, God has only one person for each of us, the identity of this person will be revealed in time, and life will be miserable if you marry someone else. Clearly, 1 Corinthians 7 teaches that marriage and singleness are both acceptable to God and the choice of a mate is governed only by the requirement that Christians must marry Christians. Beyond that, it would appear that a Christian is free to choose a marriage partner based on his or her own careful thinking and the thoughtful input of sensitive other people, including parents or a Christian counselor.

CHAPTER 10

Causes of Good and Poor Mate Selection

Choosing a marriage partner can be a difficult experience, especially in societies where the choice mostly depends on the couple. Often young, inexperienced, and blinded by infatuation and sexual attraction, it is easy for many people to make choices that later prove to be unwise. As a result, their marriages are miserable, and so are their lives and the lives of any children who may be conceived. Knowing this, some people are afraid, unwilling, or at least reluctant to take the risks of choosing a mate and building a marriage.

For most unmarried people in the world, this is not a problem. They are like a young international student at University of Kentucky who was twenty-four when his parents called from India. They told their son, Yogesh Shulkla, that they had selected a wife for him and wanted him to return home for the wedding. As a dutiful son who would not think of displeasing his parents, the young man packed his bags and went home, where he married a young woman named Sarita, whom he had never met. Today, the couple is happily together in a marriage that their parents carefully arranged. One report suggests that as many as 96 percent of the marriages in India and 60 percent of marriages worldwide are arranged. The procedures for arranging a marriage vary from one religion to another and differ from place to place, depending on the norms of the culture or subculture. The matchmaking process usually is thorough, detailed, and well established. Today, more than in generations past, the prospective husband and wife often are involved in the selection, and they even may have the freedom to veto the parental choice. After the wedding, some arranged marriages become abusive and filled with great unhappiness, although many arranged marriages work out very well. For people like

Yogesh and Sarita, there always was the expectation that their parents would handle that for them.

In contrast to marriages that parents arrange, choosing a mate based on desire and building a marriage on love are relatively recent concepts even in the Western world. Many of the early Catholic and reformation Protestant church leaders were skeptical about the single person's right to freely choose a mate. There was a general view that parents should have the major role in mate selection, and very often, marriage was not about love or happiness. It was about a political or economic arrangement between two families. More than any others, the twentieth century liberalized attitudes toward marriage and marriage selection. Probably, most of us would agree that it is best to let individuals and couples make their choice, but this can lead to considerable anxiety. To help people choose wisely and lessen the risk of making a mistake, counselors might consider five important questions:

1. **Why do people choose a marriage partner?** Despite the prevalence of arranged marriages in other parts of the world, in Western cultures, most people get married because they are in love. But love can be a confusing and ambiguous word to human beings. But this emotional high cannot and does not last by itself forever. For deep love to persist and grow, there must be a giving, other-centered relationship similar to that described in 1 Corinthians 13. It may be that, for most people, deep and secure love comes after marriage rather than before. (That has been the experience of Yogesh and Sarita from India.) To be in love, therefore, is to experience a state of emotional exhilaration; to grow in love is to involve oneself deliberately in acts of giving and caring. A feeling of being in love is not in itself a solid basis for marriage. (And neither is the fact that "we don't love each other anymore" a basis for divorce.) The biblical marriages, like marriage in many countries today, were based on issues other than feelings, and even in our society, it is probable that person really marries for reasons other than love. The reasons may be diverse, but often they center on the idea of needs. One theory of mate selection, for example, claims that opposites attract and single people are drawn to potential partners who can meet their needs by supplementing their areas of weakness. Initially, of course, loving relationships form between people who are alike in many social and cultural ways, but at a deeper level, it may be that a dominant

person is attracted to someone who is less dominant or an introvert may choose a person who is extroverted. More accepted is the broader view that marriage meets mutual needs for companionship, security, support, intimacy, friendship, and sexual fulfillment. In addition, some marry because of premarital pregnancy, social pressure from friends or parents, the desire to escape from an unhappy home environment, a fear one will be left alone, a rebound reaction to the breakup of a prior engagement, or a compulsion to rescue some unfortunate single person. Each of these reasons for marriage meets some need, although none in itself can be the basis for a mature and stable relationship. No doubt you have noticed that some of these reasons for selecting a mate are immature and self-centered; others are more rational and may result from mutual deliberation and respect. In all of this, it is wise to remember that people marry, ultimately, because God created us male and female, instituted marriage for companionship, mutual support, and sexual expression, and declared in his Word that marriage is honorable. This must not be forgotten as we help people struggle through the choice of a marriage partner.

2. **Why do some people not choose a marriage partner?** The same God who created marriage apparently did not expect that everyone would find a mate. An unmarried apostle Paul wrote that singleness should be considered a superior state because the unmarried person can be free to "serve the Lord best with as few distractions as possible." Some people remain single, therefore, because they believe this is the will and calling of God for their lives. There are other and probably more common reasons why some people do not marry.

    a. There is the failure to meet eligible partners because more are not around. In addition, most people want a mate who has similar interests or education, but many people who desire marriage may not be able to find such compatible prospects. Consider, for example, the believer who wants a Christian mate but lives in an area where there are few believers who want Christians present. The desire for marriage may be strong, but the prospects are not.
    b. Some people fail to take advantage of the opportunities that are present. Busy with education, career building, travel, or other activities, these people decide to postpone marriage, but eventually, the number of prospects declines. Others have high expectations

but keep waiting for someone better and discover too late that they have passed by some excellent opportunities for marriage.

c. Nobody likes to mention this, perhaps, but people in a third category stay single because they are unattractive to those of the opposite sex. Other things being equal, people who are looking for a mate prefer to find somebody who is physically attractive. Probably more often, psychological characteristics drive others away. Single people who are excessively timid, afraid of the opposite sex, too aggressive or loud, insensitive, socially inappropriate in their dress and mannerisms, or self-centered often cannot relate well in dating. The individual who is overly aggressive or appears too eager to get married very often scares off and drives away potential mates. In contrast, some single people are reluctant to get involved with anyone who is so passive that he or she gives the impression of not being interested in pursuing the relationship. There are a number of research studies on mate selection, some of which view the process as an exercise in self-marketing. They may not think this way, but in many ways, individuals looking for a mate present themselves and their attributes in as positive a light as possible. They seek to find the best partner they can get for what they have to offer in return. It is not surprising that people who place dating advertisements in newspapers and magazines are presenting themselves in a positive light and indicating what they are looking for in a dating relationship or prospective mate. One research team reviewed a number of these advertisements and found that men most often market their financial and occupational resources, while women still tend to describe their physical attractiveness and appealing body shape. The personal advertisements also reflect cultural differences. Whereas Americans value independence and individualism, Chinese singles emphasize their commitment to family and society. Another study compared "mates preferences" over a fifty-year period and found that both men and women mentioned their interest in mutual attractiveness, and both (especially men) were interested in whether a potential mate had domestic skills. When one group of college students posted information about themselves on an Internet mate selection site, 40 percent later admitted to researchers that they had lied online in an effort to look better. It seems probable that self-descriptions in newspaper and magazine advertisements are distorted as well. All of this suggests that they are self-marketing themselves poorly.

d. There is a failure of some people to achieve emotional independence, and this reduces their prospects for marriage. An unusually strong dependence upon one's parents or guilt over leaving a parent can cause one to remain single. This can be a commendable choice when responsible people make the deliberate but often difficult choice to remain single because of the duty to care for needy family members. Of course, sometimes even this can be an excuse to keep them from taking the risks of entering a marriage and building intimacy.

3. **Where do people find mates?** Several decades of research has confirmed that most people select mates from people who are of a similar age, education, social class, economic or income level, religion, race, and place of residence. This is changing as travel and cross-cultural communication both get easier. People often cross racial, religious, and other barriers, and many are able to build successful marriages despite their different backgrounds. But crossovers can bring pressure that makes marital adjustment more difficult. Within recent years, for example, increasing numbers of women have been marrying younger men. Often, these are good relationships except for the issue of children. Older women tend to be involved in careers and are less willing to have children. Their husbands, in contrast, are more inclined to want families. This can create tension. In looking for a mate, therefore, most people try to find someone who is of similar background and social-religious-educational level. Within this broad category, one's personal standards, parental approval or disapproval, and an individual's mental image of an ideal mate narrows the choices. Because few people can measure up to these great expectations, there often must be a relaxing of one's standards, a willingness to accept the less desirable characteristics in a potential mate, or a decision to remain single in hopes that an ideal person will eventually come along. Guided by a mental image of what they might be looking for, many unmarried people go about their daily activities with at least some alertness to the single people who might be seen, met, or befriended at school, work, church, social and athletic gatherings, conferences,

or neighborhood. Sometimes, a couple will meet as casual friends or work associates, and a more personal relationship begins to build later. In addition to this more casual way of meeting prospective mates, the Internet has given rise to online mate selection services. A Christian clinical psychologist designed a highly sophisticated relationship personality profile with 436 questions built around twenty-nine categories, including self-concept, emotional energy, sexual passion, personality traits, communication style, spirituality, beliefs, values, and family background. Participants take the questionnaire, and in exchange for a fee, the site matches them to others with whom there is the highest level of compatibility. Promoters of these services often proclaim their effectiveness enthusiastically, but researchers aren't so convinced. Preliminary investigations question the scientific validity of some of the questionnaires, and there is concern about people lying when they complete the matchmaking questionnaires. To date, there are no published studies on the stability of the marriages that result from Internet matches.

4. **Why do some people choose unwisely?** Choosing a mate is one of life's most important decisions. It involves emotions and passions, but it also needs to involve our brains, lest we make foolish choices that we will regret later. Social pressures, the influence of parents and friends, sexual urges, or strong desires to get married are among the influences that edge people into unhealthy relationships. In addition, almost everybody brings expectations to their marriages, and these may face abrupt challenges when reality appears. Sometimes, single people look for a mate solely on the basis of what they can receive without giving. They are headed for disappointment. The lopsided desire to receive, without giving, is a mark of immaturity that is rarely seen in more stable marriages where needs are met as each spouse gives to the other. With a few minutes of reflection, most of us could list reasons why people make unwise marital choices. Future tensions almost always will arise if somebody chooses a marriage partner primarily to escape a difficult home situation, prove that one is an adult, rebel against parents or a former partner, escape the stigma of being single, get an in-house sexual partner, bolster self-esteem, improve social status, or find somebody to take care of him or her. Other circumstances that signal potential problems include wide age differences, recent mental illness in one or both individuals, evidence of financial irresponsibility

and instability, substance abuse in one or both of the partners, differing religious beliefs, or wide cultural or obvious racial differences. Or there may be participants who have never dated anyone other than the intended mate. Good marriages can occur despite obstacles like these, but when several are present or when a couple appears to have unhealthy motives for choosing a mate, the choice is likely to be regretted later.

5. **Why do some choose wisely?** Despite all of the potential for failure, many people make wise choices of a marriage partner. There can be several reasons for this.

    a. **Similar religious convictions.** In Western cultures, most people first get to know their future mates through dating. Because one never knows when a dating relationship may lead to marriage, it is wise for unmarried Christian persons to limit their dating to other believers. Christians who choose wisely often pray about mate selection, at first alone and later as a couple. This principle may be of less interest to people for whom religious beliefs or spirituality are not important, but even here, it would seem that couples are more likely to be compatible if they share similar beliefs and values.

    b. **Similar backgrounds and complementary needs.** We have seen that marriage selection is best when the man and woman are similar in things such as age, interests, values, socioeconomic level, and education. In addition, it is helpful if the couple can meet each other's needs. Try, however, to distinguish between complementary and contradictory needs. Complementary needs fit so well together that a relationship is smooth and compromise is rarely needed. Contradictory needs clash and require frequent resolution. If both people enjoy social contacts but one person is outgoing and the other is a little shy, this can be complementary. In contrast, if one person loves parties and the other prefers to remain at home, these contradictory needs make conflict more likely.

    c. **Emotional resonance.** Single people sometimes wonder how they will know when the right one comes along. It isn't helpful to give the common answer, "You'll just know," but some relationships do feel harmonious and right. To use another cliché, in good relationships, there is good chemistry between the couple. With other relationships, the spark isn't there. To choose a mate on the basis of such feelings alone would surely be unwise, but to ignore one's feelings or overlook the fact that there are no feelings of attraction also would be a mistake.

d. **Compatible personalities.** Counselors sometimes write about the importance of a potential husband and wife having compatible personalities. Sometimes called "marriage ability traits," these characteristics might include the following:
   - an ability to work through problems and to persist until there is some resolution
   - flexibility
   - similar spiritual interests
   - common beliefs and values
   - a willingness to share intimate thoughts and feelings
   - emotional stability
   - good communication skills
   - appreciation for each other
   - a good sense of humor
   - the ability to give and receive love
   - comfort in expressing emotions

A survey of seven hundred twenty-year-olds found that most were looking for people who had warmth, kindness, openness, a good sense of humor, physical attractiveness, good social status, positive personality traits, and what the researchers termed "expressivity." Another research team reported that the physical attractiveness of the woman in the relationship was more important than personality in predicting good marital interactions. Other research found that "people are happiest in their relationships when they believe they have found a kindred spirit, someone who understands them and shares their experiences." In time, if it becomes apparent that the similarities are not as common as once thought, partners in good relationships tend to downplay the differences and see positive characteristics in their partners that may not be evident to other people. This may give a hint to the well-known tendency for people in love to see idealized traits in each other. Apparently, this self-deception and idealization of a partner can last into marriage and even increase marital stability. Whether or not this happens, it is good to remember that nobody can meet all of the ideal marriage traits that we assume to be of importance. For mate selection, a feeling of love or a strong urge to get married cannot be the sole basis for making a wise choice. The outside perspective and guidance of a friend or counselor can be helpful and important if one is to attain subsequent marital stability and happiness.

Effects of Good and Poor Mate Selection

Good choices do not always lead to good marriages, but careful selection of a partner does give a solid foundation on which to build a husband-wife relationship. Marriage involves effort, risk, and times of difficulty and disappointment. These never are easy experiences, but it is more pleasant and motivating to work in partnership with a compatible teammate in life than someone who apparently was the wrong choice.

Many people, however, make choices that, in retrospect, seem to have been unwise, but the couple determines nevertheless to build the best relationship possible considering the circumstances. This is what Sarita and Yogeash Shukla were prepared to do, had their parents not been so successful in arranging the marriage. People who determine to make their marriages succeed discover that loving actions often create loving feelings. In time, relatively good marriages can result.

In contrast, other people never recover from poor mate selection. Unhappiness and conflict characterize the marriage, and the relationship is dissolved emotionally, if not legally, through separation and divorce.

PART 4

How to Let Go of Someone You Love Who Doesn't Treat You Right

CHAPTER 11

How to Let Go of Someone You Love Who Doesn't Treat You Right

Sometimes it can be difficult for one partner in a relationship to let the other partner go, even if he or she has treated the other badly. This can be especially difficult while still in love with that person. Nonetheless, if a relationship becomes verbally or physically abusive, it's crucial to let go and move on. Without this, the negative cycle of behavior is likely to continue. The following five guidelines should help most people effectively cut ties with an abusive partner and move on:

1. **Remember the negative aspects of the person and the hurt he or she has caused.** In many cases, it's quite common for a partner to focus on the positive qualities of a person, which usually leaves that person in a state of limbo. Keep reminding yourself of how hurtful he or she has been to help you objectify your view of him or her and initiate the process of moving on.
2. **Realize that his or her behavior isn't going to change; force yourself to see through the deception so you can move on.** Don't believe your partner's excuses or promises that he or she will change. When you're in love, it's easy to be fooled into believing that these statements are legitimate. Remind yourself that, in most cases, the behavior never changes.
3. **Tell him or her directly that you want him out of your life and you must move on.** Be completely clear with him or her about your choice. Don't sugarcoat it or be overly nice about the situation. Be direct about your choice. You should also separate yourself from your

partner as much as possible. Maintaining contact will only make the separation process more difficult.

4. **Accept it will take a period of time to get your life back on track.** The process of letting go of any type of love takes time. Remind yourself that you're making the right choice and doing what's best for you.
5. **Work on yourself, and take time to reflect.** Don't feel guilty or beat yourself up about the situation. Remember that you're doing what's in your best interest, so try to be stabilized and begin improving your life. Over time, your life should get back on track, and you will be ready to begin new, healthier relationships.

CHAPTER 12
Conflict and Relationship

Human beings are social creatures. At the time of creation, God declared it was not good for us to be alone, so he gave Adam a companion, instructed the human race to multiply, and has permitted us to expand into the billions of people who now occupy planet Earth.

Whenever two or more of these people get together, there are interpersonal relations. Often these relationships are compatible, mutually supportive, respectful, and characterized by clear, concise, and efficient communication. At other times, conflict strains and marks interpersonal relations. There are cultural differences around the world, but at least in Western countries, most twenty-first-century people value individualism, independence, self-determination, and personal freedom. These values can be motivating, but they also cut us off from other people and make us more insensitive, lonely, and unable to get along with one another.

THE BIBLE'S GUIDING LIGHT ABOUT CONFLICT AND INTERPERSONAL RELATIONS

The Bible records a long human history of interpersonal problems and communication breakdowns. Adam and Eve, the first married couple, had a disagreement about the reasons for their sin in the Garden of Eden. Their first two sons had a conflict that led one to murder the other. Then as its population multiplied, violence filled the Earth. The Bible reports the arguments between the herdsmen of Abram and Lot, the conflicts between Joseph and his brothers, the jealousy that led Saul to be at odds with David, and the disagreement between Job and his three friends.

Although the Bible records many examples of interpersonal conflict, this is never condoned. On the contrary, dissension and interpersonal strife are dealt with honestly, and principles for building or maintaining good relationships are mentioned frequently. The book of Proverbs, for example, instructs us to hold tongues and avoid slander, tell the truth, speak gently, think before we talk, listen carefully, resist the temptation to gossip, avoid flattery, and trust in God. Unrestrained anger, hasty words, personal pride, dishonesty, envy, the struggle for riches, and a host of other harmful attributes are mentioned as sources of tension. There is no book in the Bible that equals Proverbs in clear, consistent teaching about good relationships among people.

Teaching about relationships does occur elsewhere, however. Much of the Sermon on the Mount concerns interpersonal relations. Throughout his later ministry, Jesus taught about conflict resolution, and he intervened in several disputes. Paul warned Timothy not to be quarrelsome, especially over unimportant things. And in other Bible passages, there are instructions to live in harmony, demonstrate love, and replace bitterness and wrath with kindness, forgiveness, and tenderhearted actions. After a warning against those who cause trouble because they do not control their tongues, James notes that quarrels and conflicts come because of personal lusts and envy. In listing practical guidelines for living, Paul instructs his readers to "never pay back evil for evil to anyone," to live in much harmony with each other, and to "do your part to live at peace with everyone as much as possible." Jesus and the biblical writers were peacemakers who dealt with conflict in a straightforward way, but they taught by their example and words. They expected believers to be peacemakers as well.

As we ponder the many biblical statements about conflict and interpersonal relations, several themes are apparent. Good relationships begin with Jesus Christ, depend on people, face issues honestly, and involve determination and skill. Relationship issues also can build maturity.

Good Relationships and Conflict Resolution Begin with Jesus Christ

Isaiah called Him the Prince of Peace, and at His birth, hosts of angels sang glory to God in the Highest and proclaimed, "Peace on earth to all whom God favors." During his ministry, he predicted that tension would arise between his followers and their nonbelieving relatives and friends, but he was described as a maker of peace who is able to break down interpersonal barriers and the walls of hostility that divide people.

Further, the followers of Jesus have been promised a supernaturally produced inner peace of mind that gives internal stability, even in times of turmoil and interpersonal tension. Peace with God comes to people who pray about everything, put their trust in God, ask Him to take control of their lives, and expect He will give the peace that the word of God promises. This peace, in turn, can bring calm in times of interpersonal dissension.

Despite these biblical promises, all of us still worry at times, and Christians have conflicts with each other and nonbelievers. This leads to other biblical statements about interpersonal relations.

Good Interpersonal Relations Depend on People

Relationships can be maintained, and conflicts can be managed, when people are willing to work together to resolve their differences. Counselors are among those who serve as mediators, sometimes helping with negotiations between individuals in conflict, including married couples, political factions, church members who disagree with others, or protagonists in labor disagreements. Some people are specialists in guiding negotiations between people in legal disputes or even helping to resolve conflict between nations. Although these efforts at peacemaking often can be helpful, the Bible often puts greater emphasis on the attitudes and characteristics of the persons involved in the disagreements.

In the first letter to the Corinthians, Paul appears to divide people into three categories:

- **People who aren't Christians.** There are individual differences, of course, and many are morally upright people, but as a group, they are more prone to sexual immorality, impure thoughts, eagerness for lustful pleasure, idolatry, participation in demonic activity, hostility, quarreling, jealousy, outbursts of anger, selfish ambition, and other sinful activities. These people may desire and strive for peace, but their basic alienation from God makes both inner peace and interpersonal peace more difficult to attain.
- **People who have committed their lives to Christ but have never grown spiritually.** They act like nonbelievers who are controlled by their own sinful natures and act like people who do not belong to the

Lord. They are jealous of one another and quarrel with each other. Sadly, many church members appear to be in this group, so we often see the sad spectacle of believers in conflict, sometimes in violent conflict, with their neighbors and each other. Some of these immature Christians read the Bible regularly and have good understanding of theology, but their beliefs mostly are intellectual and seem to have had little influence in their daily lives and interpersonal relationships.

- **Believers who are yielded to divine control and are seeking to think and live like Christ.** The Bible describes them as mature Christians. At times, most of these people slip back into their former worldly ways and actions, at least temporarily, but more often, their lives show increasing evidence of the "fruit of the Spirit" that involves love, joy, peace, patience, kindness, goodness, faithfulness, gentleness, and self-control.

When people are transformed within, a slow process of change begins in their outward behavior. In time, this enables them to build better interpersonal relationships.

CHAPTER 13

Establishing Strong Security in Your Relationship: Advice to Married Couples

God sees the commitment of husband and wife to each as so crucial to families that he robustly condemned any violation of that marital commitment. In the Old Testament, He said that to violate the marriage covenant is to "break faith" (NIV) or "deal treacherously" with one's spouse. With those words, He makes it clear that marriage is a covenant between husband and wife and that breaking or ending that covenant is to sin, not just against the mate, but against God himself. Look at how He words it in the book of Malachi. "Another thing you do: You flood the Lord's altar with tears. You weep and wail because He no longer pays attention to your offerings or accepts them with pleasure from your hands. You ask, 'Why?' It is because the Lord is acting as the witness between you and the wife of your youth, because you have broken faith with her, though she is your partner, the wife of your marriage covenant."

MARRIAGE COMMITMENT INCLUDES SEXUAL FIDELITY

For us, sexual faithfulness is essential. Even other people do not see it from the same angle. There is security, a special feeling of knowing you are the only one with whom your spouse chooses to have sex. I think most people, no matter what they say, can't handle affairs. When your partner has an affair, it does bad things to the other's self-esteem. An affair sends too many devastating messages: "You are not special . . . You are replaceable . . . You are not satisfying me sexually."

I believe strongly in the sanctity of marriage and hold myself to a commitment of sexual fidelity. That standard is not only wise; it is biblical. Under the Old Testament law, those who committed adultery were executed. The New Testament says, "Marriage should be honored by all, and the marriage bed kept pure, for God will judge the adulterer and all the sexually immoral."

If the Promise Is Broken

Commitment and sexual fidelity are so closely linked in most people's minds that an extramarital sexual affair is regarded as the ultimate threat to a marriage. No other enemy seems as dangerous as the other man or woman. No hurt seems as deep as betrayal by a husband or wife.

Because an extramarital affair poses such a potent threat, it is important that we briefly consider the extent of extramarital sex, the dynamics involved, and, more importantly, how strong families deal with such issues.

It's difficult to say with certainty how widespread extramarital sex is in this country. For obvious reasons, the Census Bureau has not added a question about it on its ever-expanding questionnaire. Furthermore, the dynamics of affairs are difficult to sort out. Each affair is unique. For example, some married people become involved with a stranger. Others become involved with a friend, maybe even a person who is a best friend to the couple or spouse. Some strayers have only one affair; others are chronic philanderers. Extramarital liaisons differ in duration as well, from one-night stands to long-term relationships.

There is a difference in the kind of hurt felt by those whose spouses were involved in relationship affairs and the kind of hurt felt by those whose spouses were involved in short-lived affairs. Either affair creates tremendous hurt, but greater damage was almost always experienced by those whose spouses had longer, more involved relationship affairs.

Another dynamic also comes into play. While any adultery is devastating, repeated instances of adultery are so ruinous that they create a scenario where it's almost impossible to salvage the marriage. In contrast, one-time affairs typically can be overcome if each partner is willing to do the work to get past the affair.

Obviously, for one's spiritual, emotional, familial, and material health, extramarital involvements should be avoided at all cost. Commitment to God and marriage can serve as the fortress that prevents straying.

But what if it does happen? What then?

THE END OR A NEW BEGINNING

More than a few strong relationships have dealt with extramarital sexual issues. Remember, strong relationships are not more pure than other relationships. They have problems, too. And sometimes, strong relationships have to face infidelity. But it's how strong relationships deal with their problems, including adultery, that distinguishes them from other relationships. It may surprise you to know that, for some couples who now have strong marriages, overcoming a fidelity crisis in their marriage was an important step in their long process of becoming strong.

PART 5

Missing the Plan of God for Sexuality

CHAPTER 14
Missing the Plan of God for Sexuality

Sexuality, like everything else created, has fallen into trouble. Sexual issues are one of the major conflicts in the marriage. God created sex when He made the world and created human beings. Sex was part of His plan. Sometimes, the sex problems come first and produce marital discord. More often, marital conflict or a drifting apart comes first. This generates so much anger, disappointment, resentment, fear, or tension that mutually satisfying sex no longer occurs. Regardless of which comes first, sex problems or marriage problems, sex and marriage clearly are so closely interwoven that problems in one area invariably influence the other.

ANYTHING GOD CREATED WAS GOOD

When He created human beings, He made us male and female and declared that his creation was good. He instructed the first husband and wife to "be fruitful and increase in number," instructions that clearly involved nakedness and sexual intercourse. This was not considered shameful, or at best, God tolerated it. Sex, in contrast, is evidence of God's goodness, something for which we can express praise and gratitude.

GENITAL SEXUALITY HAS THREE PURPOSES: PROCREATION, UNION, AND PLEASURE

The first birth in the Bible is described as a result of sexual intercourse plus "the help of the Lord." Obviously, sex is involved in the conception of children and the divine command to multiply. It also appears to be a fundamental way by which a husband and wife become united as "one flesh." Theologians have debated whether intercourse immediately unites a couple into one flesh and whether a couple can have a one-flesh relationship without sexual intercourse. Perhaps most would agree, however, that genital sex in marriage is a basic and important way for a couple to express commitment to the one-flesh relationship.

Is sex also intended for pleasure? Undoubtedly, the clearest answer comes from the Song of Solomon. In vivid poetic language, this little book describes the pleasures of physical sex between married lovers. The descriptions are explicit but never offensive. The same is true of Proverbs. "Rejoice in the wife of your youth . . . let her breasts satisfy you always. May you always be captivated by her love." In the New Testament, we read that husband and wife are depriving one another of sexual intimacy when they refuse to give physical pleasure and satisfaction to each other. The only exception to this is when a married couple agrees to abstain from sex temporarily and for the purpose of retreating spiritually for a special time of prayer.

Sexual Intercourse Is for Marriage

In our society, promiscuity is common, and some see sex as little more than flesh rubbing against flesh for the purpose of achieving erotic experiences. This is not true for everybody, of course, but for many people, warmth, concern, love, trust, and especially commitment are all relegated to a position that is of secondary importance to the sensations that come from foreplay and orgasm. This part draws on research of writers who study sex between unmarried partners, but the emphasis here is on sex between marriage partners who have committed themselves to each other in a marriage relationship. When the Bible speaks approvingly about sex, it refers to intercourse between married couples. Quoting Genesis, Jesus spoke with favor about the permanence and "one flesh" nature of marriage. Paul noted that marriage (not intercourse outside of marriage) is the desirable answer for a person who is struggling with sexual self-control. When marriage occurs, the husband and wife are to give their bodies freely to each other and not to hold sexually.

Sexual Immorality Is Condemned Strongly

King David was doing nothing original when he had sex with Bathsheba while her husband was away and then tried to hide what they had done. Psalms 32 and 51 are among several that describe the anguish that followed, including the grief that came when the child of this union died. When God commanded us to abstain from sexual immorality, this was not because He wanted to take away our fun. He wants to protect us from the misery that comes when we give in to lustful passions and accept the self-centered sexual values of people who neither know nor respect God's Word. The Bible portrays adultery as something that is attractive but ultimately foolish and destructive.

In contrast, the biblical view of sex within marriage is affirmed enthusiastically. Married couples are free to engage in sex as often as they want. This does not give couples freedom to use methods that would not be honoring to God in any way.

CHAPTER 15

Preventing the Next Generation: Sex Apart from Marriage

Spirituality and sexuality are two fundamental forces in life that cannot be ignored. Both can bring wonder and amazement, euphoria, physical and emotional arousal, a closeness to others, and a sense of God's presence. Both can be horribly distorted and a source of misery. Both can be used to manipulate others or to bring great fulfillment in life. The prevention of immoral, unfulfilling, and unhealthy sexual behavior can focus on two overlapping goals: providing accurate sex education and helping people find realistic alternatives to uncontrolled sexuality.

PROVIDING ACCURATE SEX EDUCATION

Most educators and parents would agree that sex education should occur at home; many agree that sex education can be taught in the schools. But what about the role of the church in sex education?

The church can influence sex education in several ways, indirectly through sermons, classes, discussions groups, and retreats. This teaching must involve giving factual information, but of equal importance is teaching biblically based principles of morality. The teaching must be honest, practical, and in good taste. To be sure it is accurate, do not hesitate to bring in resource persons, such as a physician or psychologist who can give specialized information. To ensure the relevance of the information, encourage honest questioning, and try to avoid pat answers. Written questions submitted anonymously can be one way to uncover real issues. For some, there is value in recommending books that connect with younger people and provide accurate information.

Whatever one might feel about sex education in the school, church, or home, it is important to recognize that young people hear, talk, and think a lot about sex. They learn from peers, pornography, the media, and adults, including school officials who distribute contraceptives on the dubious assumption that young people are not capable of controlling their own sexual appetites. Many unmarried people themselves who are embracing abstinence challenge this view. The church should be actively involved in helping young people say no to immoral sex.

Helping Young People Decide about Practical Issues That Deal with Self-Control

Although the Bible discusses premarital and extramarital sex, other practical sexual issues are not even mentioned, including dating and the act of masturbation.

Dating and Petting

Dating, the relationship between two people of the opposite sex, provides mutual human companionship, better understanding of the opposite sex, greater self-understanding, sexual stimulation, and some sexual fulfillment. The rules and practices of dating vary from place to place, and touching communicates interest, compassion, empathy, and affection. However, in many cases, touch is much more sensual in nature and intended to bring sexual arousal. The term *petting* may not be used as much as it was previously, but it refers to sexual touching that does not involve intercourse. Petting may involve little more than hugging and kissing, but often it refers to conscious mutual physical stimulation and exploration designed to bring erotic arousal through the fondling of sexually excitable areas of the body. For those who see no harm in no marital sex, petting is no problem. If it becomes a form of foreplay that leads to sexual intercourse, as it often does, this is acceptable to the parties involved.

But what should be the attitude and behavior of couples who believe that intercourse should be confined to marriage? Can there be responsible petting that expresses intimacy and exists for mutual discovery and sexual gratification apart from intercourse? Some Christians say no and argue for minimal physical contact, but most single Christians seem to show by their actions that their answer is yes. The church often gives no guidance in this significant area. Perhaps this is because there are no easy answers to questions about dating and petting, but several prevention conclusions can be helpful:

- God created sexual attractiveness and sexual feelings, and they should be considered good, not sinful.
- All persons, male and female, are created in God's image, and each should be respected. To use another person to satisfy one's own sexual desires is to violate that person's personhood, making him or her an object.
- God wants His people to live holy lives. Whatever they do should be done toward the glory of God.
- Christians must respect God's directions for expressing sexuality. The Bible warns against the misuse of sex, which includes anything that is done contrary to be revealed as the word of God.
- From God's perspective, the only proper place for sexual intercourse is within the context of a mutual, lifelong commitment of a man and woman, in the form of marriage. God has our best interests in view when he commands us to wait for intercourse until we are married.
- Petting is a common activity among people who are not married to each other. Unlike foreplay, a tender preparation for sexual intercourse, petting is a tender exploration of one another by two people who do not intend to have intercourse.
- Petting has many risks, spiritual and psychological. The law of diminishing returns illustrates one adverse effect of heavy petting. With constant repetition over period of time, the effect of a stimulus on an individual tends to decrease. To keep the original effect, the stimulation must be increased. Petting is a physical stimulation that conforms to this law. After reaching a certain point of intimacy, a couple almost always finds that retreat to less intimate involvement proves very difficult. In contrast, petting creates the desire for more intimate sexual union. In advanced stages, petting is especially difficult to stop and may result in frustration, tenseness, irritability, and decreasing self-control.

- God, through His Holy Spirit, is the source of personal, practical power to help us guide and control our sexuality. Sex needs not be a drive that enslaves, but it is an appetite we can feed, sometimes illicitly. For those who seek His help, God will cleanse us on a moment-by-moment basis to keep us from wrong attitudes and actions.

These are preventive principles that counselors and church leaders can communicate, sometimes in public presentations, followed by discussion.

MASTURBATION

The stimulation of one's own genitals (usually but not necessarily to the point of orgasm) is a very common form of sexual arousal apart from marriage, especially in males. The frequency of masturbation declines following adolescence and marriage, but it does not disappear. Many married men and some women continue to masturbate at times throughout their lives, and it does not appear that religious people or church attenders masturbate less frequently than others do.

There is no medical evidence to indicate that the practice is harmful to the body or that it interferes with subsequent sexual intercourse. Unlike fornication and adultery, masturbation is never mentioned in the Bible, so opinions differ about whether the practice is wrong. While some condemn masturbation, others argue it is not much of an issue with God because He never mentioned it. Probably, most would agree that masturbation is not wrong in these examples:

- A married man masturbates when his wife is ill or recovering from a pregnancy.
- A couple cannot have sexual intercourse because the husband is away on a business trip.
- A couple agrees to refrain temporarily from intercourse but agrees that masturbation is acceptable as an alternative to more intimate sex.

Is masturbation wrong when a single high school, college, or seminary student with an intense sex drive seeks to keep from engaging in no marital sexual intercourse practices it? It is widely agreed that lustful thoughts, which in themselves are wrong, most often accompanies masturbation.

Many men stimulate their minds with mental fantasies or pornographic imagery to accompany their masturbation, and these practices violate the biblical principle that we should focus our minds on what is good, doing all to the glory of God. Because masturbation has a way of growing in frequency and intensity, it can become a compulsive habit that violates biblical principles and is very difficult to forsake even within the bonds of a subsequent marriage. Unsurprisingly, feelings of guilt, frustration, or self-condemnation accompany masturbation. Many feel angry and discouraged because of its compulsive grip. Some may be like the members of a Christian college group, trying to eliminate pornography, lust, and masturbation from our lives and wondering if there were any special way to masturbate without sinning.

Those who masturbate should understand the biblical perspective on sex and marriage. Masturbation clearly is a substitute activity. Prayer and a sincere willingness to let the Holy Spirit be in control can reduce masturbation. Understanding the biblical perspective on sex and marriage may also help to control masturbation.

CHAPTER 16
Preventing Pregnancy Problems

To prevent premarital pregnancies, young people need sex education that includes moral guidelines and practical help in learning and applying abstinence and self-control. To prevent abortion, there needs to be better education about abortion procedures, post-abortion trauma and grief, and alternative ways to cope with unwanted pregnancy. If prevention is to be effective, each of these general suggestions must be adapted to individuals. In addition, there can be prevention that focuses on sex, support, and suffering.

SEX

This has caused intense pleasure and incredible misery since the beginning of the human race. One poignant Old Testament drama concerns a young man named Amnon, David's son, who was so much in love that others noted his haggard look. Through a series of shrewd moves, including deception, Amnon was able to get alone with the woman for whom he had so much attraction, and when she resisted his sexual advances, he raped her. "Then suddenly Amnon's love turned to hate, and he hated her even more than he had loved her. 'Get out of here!' he snarled at her." The young man's intense sexual urges had led to forced intercourse, followed by regret, injustice, family problems, and death.

Out-of-control sexual urges have always led to regrettable consequences. Some cultures are less tolerant of the blatant sexuality that we in the West find paraded before us on television; in various forms of entertainment, including movies; and in advertising, business, education, and sometimes religious circles. Even in cultures where sexuality is more discretely hidden,

Internet sexuality breaks through to reach anybody who wants it. None of us should find it surprising that, with all of this stimulation, many people fall into sexual sin, followed by personal regret and increasing numbers of unwanted pregnancies, many of which end in abortion.

Realistic and sensitive sex education that includes accurate information, clear teaching about biblical morality, and practical guidance to help people maintain self-control must counter this. The focus of this education may be on the young as opposed to the more popular self-centered sexuality.

PART 6

Building a Strong Family

CHAPTER 17
Building a Strong Family

The family plays a very important role in our society. We realized all the good and bad would come from families. It is very important to focus on the center of all, which is the family. Unfortunately, the family is lying down in the hospital bed suffering from an unknown disease, but we could find a cure. Analyzing the specimen, all the tests revealed negative. It's a very delicate case. All the specialists are trying their best methods: seminars, counseling, conferences, family meetings, and parenting classes. But they do not get the best result yet. The solution seems complicated but is very simple. They need to go back to the original, to the true source. God created the first family, and the method to use and resolve the complication in the union of two is "one flesh."

"Therefore shall a man leave his father and his mother, and cleave unto his wife: and shall be one flesh" (Gen. 2:24). "One" as the number of God means unity. A house divided will be destroyed. When we put all the laws of God aside, we cannot expect wonders. The word of God says, "Submit yourselves unto one another in the fear of God. Wives submit yourselves unto your own husband, as unto the Lord" (Eph. 5:21–22), so men ought to love their wives as their own bodies. He who loves his wife loves himself. For no man ever yet hated his own but nourished and cherished it, even as the Lord the church. We're all created for a purpose to reflect the glory of God and manifest in our daily work. The first family failed to fulfill its calling by compromising the word of God and listening to the enemy's opinion about what God had said to them.

In your relationship, don't open the door to the devil to come and destroy your union. He is the promoter of division. God had to rescue the first family, Adam and Eve, in order for us to live the best life now. God says to Satan, "I will put enmity between thee and the woman, and between thy seed and her seed; it shall bruise thy head, and thou shall bruise his heel" (Gen. 3:15).

Hope for Families

The precious blood of Jesus has reversed the curse. We should rise up the standard of integrity and bring back the glory into our household, our community, and our society. Our Christians families must be the light to show the way to the world, to give hope to the hopeless. Many teens are involved in drugs, prostitution, crimes, violence, and much more, but it is a shame to know their background. Most are the seed of promise. Their parents are in church, and the children are in jails or on the street. For some I've had a chance to talk to, their parents are either separated or divorced. Family, wake up. You let the enemy in. While more than 60 percent of the world's population is under twenty-five years of age, the number of casualties among them is alarming. Drugs, sex, and crime have twisted their minds and drained their bodies. The next generation will not be fathered by persuasive pulpiteers and public orators, but by committed adults who will spend time with their children, imparting life both by instruction and example. Remember God says that you and your children have everything you need for a godly life and cannot fail (2 Pet. 1:3). I have a true story about a group, a gang. They've committed a horrible crime. On their judgment day, many people were there to assist their sentence.

A journalist asked one of them, "What would we do for you to stop the violence and put the guns down?"

One of them answered, "Just give us a family because those boys are the only I got."

Someone must have done something horrible to those young boys or let them down. Folks, something needs to be done before it is too late. Some people might say, "That's not my concern because our family has it all together." But our society needs all of us to make a positive impact in the lives of other families. Let us use our Christ, Prevention, and Restoration (CPR) team to revive the dry bones of the family and bring them back again to rebuild the temple of God, our community, and our society. We all Christians have our part of responsibility to bring the change, the restoration, and the peace.

Our families need to stand on the solid foundation. Jesus, the chief of the family, loves the true foundation of the family. The family that keeps communicating has mutual respect. They share ideas and feelings. They provide safety, support, and trust. They are honest and spend time together. If the family is the center of all, they should remain firm after the adversities and trials. Let us save our heritage. We need a better society, but the cleanup must start individually and will give birth to new families, new communities, and new societies. We must apply the method of "one flesh." We are the light of the world, allowing them to see through us as the manifestation of His glory in our lives by being an example, a role model family as God designed it from the foundation of this earth. "Yet, we are the salt of the world. If salt have lost his savor wherewith shall it be salted?" (Matt. 5:13–14). The truth of eternality also demands that things be reformed, reborn, and restored to former and/or future vitality, purpose, and image. For this to take place, there must be an absolute standard of truth, a hallmark for integrity, and a divine understanding of the concept of wholeness. Man has been created superior and given dominion, authority, and the mandate for stewardship of the earth. That domain includes the land, resources, systems, and leadership of men. He must be prepared to rise up children of destiny, who will both follow and outstrip him in the pursuit of leadership of nations. Parents, you must know your responsibility, and every family will have to answer God for the good or bad in the garden.

CHAPTER 18
The Price of Wisdom Is beyond Rubies

What is wisdom? And what is that gift of wisdom that makes a person stand superior to the rest? The gift of wisdom makes the difference and gives advantage to the wise leader. The critical advantages wise men have over foolish men provide the security, well-being, and resources that our children need. It is true to say that wisdom is the principal source of success for persons destined for success in national leadership.

Good parents eagerly hold on to God's promises for their children. The prophet Joel proclaimed a significant promise: "I will pour out my spirit upon all flesh; and your sons and your daughters shall prophesy . . . your young men shall see visions: and upon the handmaids in those days will I pour out my spirit" (Joel 2:28–29). We have taken this promise for ourselves. However, our children will outstrip us. They will be infused with a supernatural giftedness so they will execute extraordinary feats. They will be endowed with abilities needed for national leadership.

What is the role and work of the Spirit in the lives of our children? The prophet Isaiah declared a similar blessing for our seed, demonstrating God's unchanging intention to raise up seed filled with wisdom: "I will pour my Spirit upon thy seed, and my blessing upon thine offspring" (Isa. 44:3).

Even earlier than the prophecies of the prophets Joel and Isaiah, the cry of wisdom echoed God's desire and longing: "Behold, I [wisdom] will pour out my spirit unto you, I will make known my words unto you" (Prov. 1:23). The earliest existence of the spirit of wisdom is evidenced in the wonders of the created universe. The absolute perfection of the functioning of universal principles and laws declares the role of wisdom.

Wisdom is God's provision for the extension of life to the young. It is the creative force of God, existing with Him before and during creation, yet still sustaining life.

The cry of wisdom reveals a truth that is crucial to the fulfillment of purpose in our children of promise. It is wisdom personified in Christ that cries out, "I will pour out My Spirit unto you." The entire book of Proverbs contains hundreds of practical teachings that will bring life to every young person who will follow their lead. On the other hand, if they neglect to walk in wisdom, then poverty, illness, and subsequently death becomes the sure result. Wisdom, like the heart of our Father God, cries out for all to run to receive the blessing of the spirit who brings life.

Proverbs 8 describes the activity of wisdom in the beginning, before the Earth was made. Wisdom was always with God, possessed by God, and the daily delight of God. Wisdom appears to be God's life-giving energy. "For by me thy days shall be multiplied" (Prov. 9:11). Wisdom is the craftsman, the supreme intelligence behind all physical and metaphysical laws and principles.

Wisdom begins with the decision to obey godly instruction. A life of wisdom will preserve the lives of our sons and daughters! Wisdom stands at the top of the high places and cries, "Unto you, O men, I call; and my voice is to the sons of man" (Prov. 8:4). Wisdom makes its appeal to the same sons and daughters who are targeted by a ruthless adversary who seeks to destroy them.

The opposite of a wise man is a fool. The apostle Paul described a fool by recounting the depths of sexual perversity and lawlessness of the unredeemed man. "Professing themselves to be wise, they became fools . . . who knowing the judgment of God, that they which commit such things are worthy of death, not only do the same, but have pleasure in them that do them" (Rom. 1:22, 32). Paul literally defined *foolishness* as knowing God's judgment (consequences) and still reveling in disobedience. Therefore, wisdom is the decision to obey God's law and the standards of right living. It is not only the determination to do right but also the absence of pleasure in the companionship of those who persist in doing wrong or in foolish action.

Paul also wrote, "Let the word of Christ dwell in you richly in all wisdom . . . And whatsoever ye do in word or deed, do all in the name of the Lord Jesus" (Col. 3:16–17). Wisdom is doing. It is the activity of walking out good deeds toward God, others, and one's self. It is the power or energy to do right.

PART 7

Family Manners for Kids of All Ages

Chapter 19
Family Manners for Kids of All Ages

The best time to tackle a minor problem is before it grows larger. Where there is life, there should be love, especially familial love. Love makes a house a home. Size, color, and location have nothing to do with the spirit that dwells inside. The quality or spirit they share shapes a family and its manners. A spirit based on love makes a happy home and always produces good manners. When a child feels love, understanding, and genuine recognition, many of the problems of delinquency are avoided.

Manners aren't taught in school. Children learn manners at home. They study parents. The learning process begins in the cradle. It's quickly evident that a child doesn't have to be taught to be bad. They have to be taught to be good. If a parent doesn't teach, a child will tend to go as far as he or she can—in the wrong direction. Children learn best by example. They mimic what they see. The parent who loves always teaches and trains. A lack of discipline signifies a lack of love. Many lessons in life are caught, not taught.

Second in importance to love in a family is communication. Families need to talk to each other, and they need to talk honesty. But it's not always easy to be completely honest. Some subjects are embarrassing to discuss. It might seem easier, at times, to tell a white lie and avoid the truth. Honesty is always the best policy and the best manners, especially at home.

Good manners are healthy and make us good listeners. A family can't enjoy communication if no one is listening. It may seem easier to speak up than to listen. Manners can become sloppy. We relax a bit too much. People living in close quarters can sometimes rub each other the wrong way. We're all vulnerable to hurt and upset.

Don't forget that love is a very unselfish quality of life. Don't forget all about good manners. Don't think selfishly. Look for balm rather than blame. The closeness that causes friction in a home shouldn't overshadow the closeness that makes a family. Familial love, support, and forgiveness are far greater than any hurts.

No one knows you like a brother. No one loves you like a mother. No one trusts you like a sister. No one cares for you like a father. There are two disappointments in life: not getting everything we want and getting everything we want.

It naturally hurts to be corrected or to be denied something we want very badly, but the biggest handicap parents can impose on a child is to make life too easy. A parent may need to withhold many things, but never love. A child may need to accept limits on his desires, but always in love.

Don't be discouraged if your children reject your advice. Years later, they will offer it to their own offspring. The following are some other guidelines:

- Have a positive attitude. Be cheerful and honest, and try to get along.
- Don't try to manipulate or guilt others into doing something.
- Be direct and polite when you need to discuss a conflict, whether between parent and child or among other family members. It's good training for solving conflicts encountered outside the family.
- Pitch in with chores and tasks. Keep bathrooms and common rooms clean when you leave the room. Help a little extra when someone is sick or injured.
- Ask permission before borrowing things. Promptly return them to where you found them, and return them in the same or better condition than when you borrowed them. Immediately make amends if you lose or damage something you borrowed.
- Don't insist others borrow something of yours and then resent it when they don't return the item promptly.
- Avoid disgusting habits, such as
    - picking at your face, nose, teeth, hair, beard, mustache, ears or earrings, scalp, acne, scabs, or any other body part, especially around food and drinks;
    - snorting, spitting, cracking knuckles, or passing gas;

- belching, sneezing, or coughing without covering your mouth and nose;
- clearing your throat noisily, sniffling, or blowing your nose at the table (preferably done in private in the bathroom);
- chewing gum with your mouth open;
- smoking;
- bouncing your leg up and down or vibrating your foot nervously;
- scratching yourself or brushing off dust or dandruff anywhere people prepare or eat food or drinks;
- brushing or combing your hair or applying makeup or lipstick in public; and
- resting and uncovering a bandaged wound on a counter, table, or other surface.

CHAPTER 20
Babysitting

Children are like mosquitoes. The minute they stop making noises, you know they're getting into something. As babysitters, you're in charge of much more than diapers. You're in charge of life. Babysitting is one of the most important jobs in the world. When you're asked to babysit, you're being paid far more than a fee! You're being paid a tremendous compliment. Parents are trusting you with their most valuable possessions, their children and their home.

Whether parents say it or not, they're actually telling every babysitter they believe you're honest, trustworthy, capable, responsible, intelligent, loving, qualified, and compassionate. It gives you a lot to think about, doesn't it? Don't fall short.

Before the parents leave, you need to know what exactly you're expected to do. In an emergency, you should know where the parents can be reached, a neighbor's phone number, the street address in case 911 is called, the phone numbers for fire and police if there's no 911 service, the family doctor's phone number, and where to find the child's medication for asthma, diabetes, or severe allergies.

For the older children, ask the following:

- Are they permitted to play outside? Have company?
- Are they allowed to go swimming? Should they bathe before bedtime?
- Are they to be fed? Can they watch TV? Play video games? For how long?
- Do they have any program restrictions? Is there homework? Can they have snacks?

For babies, ask the following:

- Does the baby need a bottle? Should it be warmed? How?
- Does the baby need more than a bottle? What? When? How much?
- Where are the diapers? What is the baby's bedtime routine?

HOUSE CARE

Your first responsibility is to the children, but you're also responsible for the house. You're expecting to care for both. Clean up after the children, keep toys picked up, leave the kitchen neat, and clean any dishes you use. Leave the house looking as good as or better than when you arrived. Don't use the phone, have friends in, leave the house, help yourself to food and drinks, or use any media or electronic equipment without the parents' prior permission. If someone calls for the parents, take a message. Say they cannot come to the phone, but don't reveal that you're the babysitter and the parents are not home. Write down who called, the phone number, when the call was received, and any message. Give the message to the parents when they return.

CHAPTER 21
Manners for Younger Kids

BIRTHDAY PARTIES

Birthday parties are fun! They mean presents, cards, games, friends, cake and ice cream, and all sorts of neat decorations. They also mean you're a year older and at a perfect time to display your manners.

When you are the host, spend as much time as possible with each guest at your party. Don't show any favoritism when you're the host. Greet each person, and be sure to introduce him or her to anyone he or she doesn't know. Thank each one with lots of enthusiasm for his or her gift. If you don't like a gift you receive, don't reveal it. If you already have the very same thing, don't reveal that either. It's nice to go to the door with each guest as he or she leaves. Thank him or her again for the gift. (Try to name the gift.)

When you are a guest, if the birthday child (person) answers the door, always wish him or her a happy birthday. Be sure to add his or her name as you present your birthday gift. If someone you haven't met meets you at the door, introduce yourself. Participate in all the games and enjoy them. Use all your good manners at the table and during the party. When you leave the party, thank your friend and his or her parents (if appropriate) for a special time. Leave them one of your best smiles.

Always be on time! Birthday parties are very special events. Arriving on time is polite and important. Your friend who is celebrating can't wait for the fun to begin. The parents have been filling balloons, decorating, baking a cake, and putting plenty of love and effort into all the preparations. All you have to do is to be on time and let the fun begin!

Honor Your Parents and Grandparents

Parents deserve your respect. They don't need to qualify for it. They earned it when they gave you life. Honor your parents by asking for their advice, looking at things from their perspective, trying to please them, having a good attitude, and showing respect. Thank your parents, compliment them, and obey them. Parents need your honor. They want to know they have your support, just as you want to know you have theirs.

Take out the garbage, do the dishes, and volunteers to do chores. Better yet, do chores without complaining! Have a grateful attitude and a cheerful, cooperative spirit. This will help parents the most.

Respect your grandparents. Write them. Always remember to thank them and tell them you love them.

Sisters and Brothers

We often spend more time with our sisters and brothers than we do with anyone else. We also may have more problems with them than we have with others! Manners show in the way you speak to those you love, especially the tone of your voice, the things you say and later regret, your compassion for each other, your support for those you love, and the ways you help each other.

When you feel good about yourself, you can reach out and help others. Helping others should start with your own family. Show interest, love, and concern for them. Compliment and uphold them. Root for them. Offer to help them with their chores.

PART 8

Relationship and Friendship Marketplace Open 24/7

CHAPTER 22
Food for Souls

Accept one another, then, just as Christ accepted you, in order to bring praise to God.

Romans 15:7

Carry each other's burdens, and in this way you will fulfill the law of Christ.

Galatians 6:2

Confess your sins to each other and pray for each other so that you may be healed. The prayer of a righteous person is powerful and effective.

James 5:16

Let no debt remain outstanding, except the continuing debt to love one another, for whoever loves others has fulfilled the law. The commandments . . . are summed up in this one command: "Love your neighbor as yourself." Love does no harm to its neighbor. Therefore love is the fulfillment of the law.

Romans 13:8–10

Be devoted to one another in brotherly love. Honor one another above yourselves.

Romans 12:10

Walk with wise and become wise.

Proverbs 13:20

I appeal to you . . . in the name of our Lord Jesus Christ, that all of you agree with one another so that there may be no divisions among you and that you may be perfectly united in mind and thought.

1 Corinthians 1:10

Jesus said, "A new command I give you: Love one another. As I have loved you, so you must love one another."

John 13:34

Live in harmony with one another. Do not be proud, but be willing to associate with people of low position. Do not be conceited. Do not repay anyone evil for evil. Be careful to do what is right in the eyes of everybody. If it is possible, as far as it depends on you, live at peace with everyone.

Romans 12:16–18

Let us stop passing judgment on one another. Instead, make up your mind not to put any stumbling block or obstacle in the way of a brother or sister.

Romans 14:13

Everyone should be quick to listen, slow to speak and slow to become angry.

James 1:19

You, my brothers and sisters, were called to be free. But do not use your freedom to indulge the sinful nature; rather, serve one another humbly in love. For the entire law is fulfilled in keeping this one command: "Love your neighbor as yourself." If you keep on biting and devouring each other, watch out or you will be destroyed by each other.

Galatians 5:13-15

Be completely humble and gentle; be patient, bearing with one another in love. Make every effort to keep the unity of the Spirit through the bond of peace.

Ephesians 4:2–3

Submit to one another out of reverence for Christ.

Ephesians 5:21

Bear with each other and forgive whatever grievances you may have against one another. Forgive as the Lord forgave you. And over all these virtues put on love, which binds them all together in perfect unity. Let the peace of Christ rule in your hearts, since as members of one body you were called to peace. And be thankful. Let the word of Christ dwell in you richly as you teach and admonish one another with all wisdom, and as you sing psalms, hymns and spiritual songs with gratitude in your hearts to God.

Colossians 3:13–16

Encourage one another and build each other up, just as in fact you are doing.

1 Thessalonians 5:11

Let us consider how we may spur one another on toward love and good deeds. Let us not give up meeting together, as some are in the habit of doing, but let us encourage one another—and all the more as you see the Day approaching.

Hebrews 10:24–25

Now that you have purified yourselves by obeying the truth so that you have sincere love for each other, love one another deeply, from the heart.

1 Peter 1:22

Be like-minded, be sympathetic, love one another, be compassionate and humble. Do not repay evil with evil or insult with insult. On the contrary, repay evil with blessing, because to this you were called so that you may inherit a blessing.

1 Peter 3:8–9

Offer hospitality to one another without grumbling. Each one should use whatever gift he has received to serve others.

1 Peter 5:5

Dear friends, since God so loved us, we also ought to love one another. No one has ever seen God; but if we love one another, God lives in us and his love is made complete in us.

1 John 4:11–12

Jesus said, "My command is this: Love each other as I have loved you. Greater love has no one than this: to lay down one's life for one's friends."

John 15:12–13

God has combined the members of the body and has given greater honor to the parts that lacked it, so that there should be no division in the body, but that its parts should have equal concern for each other. If one part suffers, every part suffers with it; if one part is honored, every part rejoices with it.

1 Corinthians 12:24–26

Be kind and compassionate to one another, forgiving each other, just as in Christ God forgave you. Be imitators of God, therefore, as dearly loved children and live a life of love, just as Christ loved us and gave himself up for us.

Ephesians 4:32–5:2

Friendship

I am a friend to all who fear you, to all who follow your precepts.

Psalm 119:63

The righteous choose their friends carefully, but the way of the wicked leads them astray.

Proverbs 12:26

A friend loves at all times, and a brother is born for adversity.

Proverbs 17:17

One who has unreliable friends soon comes to ruin, but there is a friend who sticks closer than a brother.

Proverbs 18:24

One who loves a pure heart and who speaks with grace will have the King for a friend.

Proverbs 22:11

Wounds from a friend can be trusted, but an enemy multiplies kisses.

Proverbs 27:6

Do not forsake your friend and the friend of your father.

Proverbs 27:10

Two are better than one, because they have a good return for their labor: If they fall down, they can help each other up. But pity those who fall and have no one to help them up! Also, if two lie down together, they will keep warm, but how can one keep warm alone? Though one may be overpowered, two can defend themselves. A cord of three strands is not quickly broken.

Ecclesiastes 4:9–12

Jesus said, "Greater love has no one than this: to lay down one's life for one's friends."

John 15:13

Perfume and incense bring joy to the heart, and the pleasantness of a friend springs from their heartfelt advice.

Proverbs 27:9

Jesus said, "You are my friends if you do what I command."

John 15:14

When Jesus saw their faith, he said, "Friend, your sins are forgiven."

Luke 5:20

Jonathan said to David, "Go in peace, for we have sworn friendship with each other in the name of the Lord, saying, "The Lord is witness between you and me, and between your descendants and my descendants forever."

1 Samuel 20:42

Dear friends, let us love one another, for love comes from God.

1 John 4:7

The scripture was fulfilled that says, "Abraham believed God, and it was credited to him as righteousness," and he was called God's friend.

James 2:23

The Lord would speak to Moses face to face, as one speaks to a friend.

Exodus 33:11

Jesus said, "I no longer call you servants, because a servant does not know his master's business. Instead, I have called you friends, for everything that I learned from my Father I have made known to you."

John 15:15

Do not make friends with the hot-tempered. Do not associate with those who are easily angered, or you may learn their ways and get yourself ensnared.

1 John 4:11

As iron sharpens iron, so one person sharpens another.

Proverbs 27:17

Walk with the wise and become wise, for a compassion of fools suffers harm.

Proverbs 13:20

Gossips betray a confidence, but the trustworthy keep a secret.

Proverbs 11:13

A gossip betrays a confidence; so avoid anyone who talks too much.

Proverbs 20:19

God, who has called you into fellowship with his Son Jesus Christ our Lord, is faithful.

1 Corinthians 1:9

Do not be yoked together with unbelievers. For what do righteousness and wickedness have in common? Or what fellowship can light have with darkness?

2 Corinthians 6:14

We proclaim to you what we have seen and heard, so that you also may have fellowship with us. And our fellowship is with the Father and his Son, Jesus Christ.

1 John 1:3

If we claim to have fellowship with him yet walk in the darkness, we lie and do not live by the truth. But if we walk in the light, as he is in the light, we have fellowship with one another, and the blood of Jesus, his Son, purifies us from all sin.

1 John 1:6–7

Be devoted to one another in love. Honor one another above yourselves.

Romans 12:10

Jesus said, "Here I am! I stand at the door and knock. If anyone hears my voice and opens the door, I will come in and eat with them, and they with me."

Revelation 3:20

Marriage

The Lord God said, "It is not good for the man to be alone. I will make a helper suitable for him." . . . The Lord God caused the man to fall into a deep sleep; and while he was sleeping, he took one of the man's ribs and closed up the place with flesh. Then the Lord God made a woman from the rib he had taken out of the man, and he brought her the man. The man said, "This is now bone of my bones and flesh of my flesh; she shall be called 'woman,' for she was taken out of man." The man and his wife were both naked; they felt no shame.

Genesis 2:18, 21–23, 25

Marriage should be honored by all, and the marriage bed kept pure.

Hebrews 13:4

Blessed are all who fear the Lord, who walk in his ways . . . Your wife will be like a fruitful vine within your house.

Psalm 128:1, 3

A wife of noble character is her husband's crown, but a disgraceful wife is like decay in his bones.

Proverbs 12:4

Wives, submit to your husbands as to the Lord. For the husband is the head of the wife as Christ is the head of the church, his body, of which he is the Savior. Now as the church submits to Christ, so also wives should submit to their husbands in everything. Husbands, love your wives, just as Christ loved the Church and gave himself up for her to make her holy, cleansing her by the washing with water through the word, and to present her to himself as a radiant church, without stain or wrinkle or any other blemish, but holy and blameless. In this same way, husbands ought to love their wives as their own bodies. He who loves his wife loves himself. After all, no one ever hated his own body, but he feeds and cares for it, just as Christ does the church—for we are members of his body. "For this reason a man will leave his father and mother and united to his wife, and the two will become one flesh."

Ephesians 5:22–31

Encourage one another and build each other up.

1 Thessalonians 5:11

A wife of noble character who can find? She is worth far more than rubies. Her husband has full confidence in her and lacks nothing of value. She brings him good, not harm, all the days of her life . . . Her husband is respected at the city gate, where he takes his seat among the elders of the land . . . Her children arise and call her blessed; her husband also, and he praises her; "Many women do noble things, but you surpass them all." Charm is deceptive, and beauty is fleeting; but a woman who fears the Lord is to be praised. Give her the reward she has earned, and let her works bring her praise at the gate.

Proverbs 31:10–12, 23, 28–31

Wives, submit to your husbands, as is fitting in the Lord.

Colossians 3:18

Houses and wealth are inherited from parents, and receive favor from the Lord.
Proverbs 19:14

He who finds a wife finds what is good and receives favor from the Lord.
Proverbs 18:22

Many waters cannot quench love; rivers cannot wash it away.
Song of Songs 8:7

Wives are to be women worthy of respect, not malicious talkers but temperate and trustworthy in everything.
1 Timothy 3:11

Drink water from your own cistern, running water from your own well. Should your springs overflow in the streets, your streams of water in the public squares? Let them be yours alone, never to be shared with strangers. May your fountain be blessed, and may you rejoice in the wife of your youth. A loving doe, a graceful deer—may her breasts satisfy you always, may you ever be captivated by her love.
Proverbs 5:15–19

I belong to my lover, and his desire is for me.
Song of Songs 7:10

If a woman has a husband who is not a believer and he is willing to live with her, she must not divorce him. For the unbelieving husband has been sanctified through his wife, and the unbelieving wife has been sanctified through her believing husband.
1 Corinthians 7:13–14

Wives . . . be submissive to your husbands so that, if any of them do not believe the word, they may be won over without words by the behavior of their wives, when they see the purity and reverence of your lives.
1 Peter 3:1–2

How good and pleasant it is when God's people live together in unity! For there the Lord bestows his blessings, even life forevermore.
Psalm 133:1, 3

Let your conversation be always full of grace.

Colossians 4:6

LOVE

I pray that you, being rooted and established in love, may have power, together with all the saints, to grasp how wide and long and high and deep is the love of Christ, and to know this love that surpasses knowledge—that you may be filled to the measure of all the fullness of God.

Ephesians 3:17–19

If you really keep royal law found in Scripture, "Love your neighbor as yourself," you are doing right.

James 2:8

We love because He first loved us.

1 John 4:19

Jesus said, "Love your enemies, do good to them, and lend to them without expecting to get anything back. Then your reward will be great, and you will be sons of the Most High."

Luke 6:35

Above all, love each other deeply, because love covers over a multitude of sins.

1 Peter 4:8

No one has ever seen God; but if we love one another, God lives in us and His love is made complete in us.

1 John 4:12

Love the Lord your God with your heart and with all your soul and with all your strength.

Deuteronomy 6:5

If anyone acknowledges that Jesus is the Son of God, God lives in them and they in God. And so we know and rely on the love God has for us. God is love. Whoever lives in love lives in God, and God in them.

1 John 4:15–16

Because of his great love for us, God, who is rich in mercy, made us alive with Christ even when we were dead in transgressions—it is by grace you have been saved.

Ephesians 2:4–5

Jesus replied, "Anyone who loves me will obey my teaching. My Father will love them, and we will come to them and make our home with them."

John 14:23

The Lord appeared to us in the past, saying: "I have loved you with an everlasting love; I have drawn you with loving kindness."

Jeremiah 31:3

Love is patient, love is kind. It does not envy, it does not boast, it is not rude, it is not self-seeking, it is not easily angered, it keeps no record of wrongs. Love does not delight in evil but rejoices with the truth. It always protects, always trusts, always hopes, always perseveres. Love never fails.

1 Corinthians 13:4–8

Many are woes of the wicked, but the Lord's unfailing love surrounds those who trust in Him.

Psalm 32:10

I am convinced that neither death nor life, neither angels nor demons, neither the present nor the future, nor any powers, neither height nor depth, nor anything else in all creation, will be able to separate us from the love of God that is in Christ Jesus our Lord.

Romans 8:38–39

This is love: not that we loved God, but that he loved us and sent his Son as an atoning sacrifice for our sins.

1 John 4:10

How great is the love the Father has lavished on us, that we should be called children of God! And that is what we are!

1 John 3:1

As high as the heavens are above the earth, so great is [God's] love for those who fear Him.

Psalm 103:11

Dear friends, let us love one another, for love comes from God. Everyone who loves has been born of God and knows God.

1 John 4:7

God is love. Whoever lives in love lives in God, and God in him. In this way, love is made complete among us so that we will have confidence on the day of judgment, because in this world we are like him.

1 John 4:16–17

In your unfailing love [Lord], you will lead the people you have redeemed. In your strength you will guide them to your Holy dwelling.

Exodus 15:13

[The Lord] passed in front of Moses, proclaiming, "The Lord, the Lord, the compassionate and gracious God, slow to anger, abounding in love and faithfulness, maintaining love to thousands, and forgiving wickedness, rebellion and sin."

Exodus 34:6–7

The lord your God is God of gods and Lord of lords, the great God, mighty and awesome, who shows no partiality and accepts no bribes. He defends the cause of the fatherless and the widow, and loves the foreigners residing among you, giving them food and clothing.

Deuteronomy 10:17–18

For everlasting to everlasting, the Lord's love is with those who fear Him, and His righteousness with their children's children.

Psalm 103:17

These three remain: faith, hope, and love. But greatest of these is love.

1 Corinthians 13:13

The Lord set his affection on your forefathers and loved them, and He chose you, their descendants, above all the nations.

Deuteronomy 10:15

Surely goodness and love will follow me all the days of my life, and I will dwell in the house of the Lord forever.

Psalm 23:6

I will be glad and rejoice in your love, for you saw my affliction and knew the anguish of my soul.

Psalm 31:7

The Lord loves righteousness and justice; the earth is full of His unfailing love.

Psalm 33:5

Kindness

The Lord is gracious and righteous; our God is full of compassions. The Lord protects the simple hearted; When I was in great need, he saved me.

Psalm 116:5–6

You, O Lord, are a compassionate and Gracious God, slow to anger, abounding in love and faithfulness.

Psalm 86:15

The Lord is good to all; He has compassion on all He has made.

Psalm 145:9

"Though the mountains be shaken and the hills be removed, yet my unfailing love for you will not be shaken, nor my covenant of peace be removed," says the Lord, who has compassion on you.

Isaiah 54:10

The Lord longs to be gracious to you; He rises to show you compassion. For the Lord is a God of Justice. Blessed are all who wait for Him!

Isaiah 30:18

Your compassion is great, O Lord; preserve my life according to your laws.

Psalm 119:156

As a father has compassion on his children, so the Lord has compassion on those who fear him.

Psalm 103:13

In a surge of anger, I hid my face from you for a moment, but with everlasting kindness I will have compassion on you, says the Lord your Redeemer.

Isaiah 54:8

"I will betroth you to me forever; I will betroth you in righteousness and justice, in love and compassion," declares the Lord.

Hosea 2:19

Because of the Lord's great love we are not consumed, for his compassions never fail. They are new every morning; great is your faithfulness.

Lamentations 3:22–23

You will again have compassion on us; You will tread our sins underfoot and hurl all our iniquities into the depths of the sea.

Psalm 112:4

Those who are kind to the poor lend to the Lord, and he will reward them for what they have done.

Proverbs 19:17

Those who are kind benefit themselves, but the cruel bring ruin on themselves.

Proverbs 11:17

Whoever is kind to the needy honors God.

Proverbs 14:31

A kindhearted woman gains respect but ruthless men gain only wealth.

Proverbs 11:16

Anxiety weighs down the heart, but a kind word cheers it up.

Proverbs 12:25

As God's chosen people, holy and dearly loved, clothe yourselves with compassion, kindness, humility, gentleness and patience.

Colossians 3:12

God's kindness leads you toward repentance.

Romans 2:4

JOY

You love righteousness and hate wickedness; therefore God, your God, has set you above your companions by anointing you with the oil of joy.

Psalm 45:7

Light is shed upon the righteous and joy on the upright in heart.

Psalm 97:11

Consider it pure joy, my brothers and sisters, whenever you face trials of many kinds, because you know that the testing of your faith produces perseverance.

James 1:2–3

Splendor and majesty are before [the Lord]; strength and joy are in his dwelling place.

1 Chronicles 16:27

The Lord your God will bless you in all your harvest and in all the work of your hands, and your joy will be complete.

Deuteronomy 16:15

Surely you have granted [the king] eternal blessings and made him glad the joy of your presence.

Psalm 21:6

You have made known to me the path of life; you will fill me with joy in your presence, with eternal pleasures at your right hand.

Psalm 16:11

The humble will rejoice in the Lord; the needy will rejoice in the Holy One of Israel.

Isaiah 29:19

The joy of the Lord is your strength.

Nehemiah 8:10

Though you have not seen [Jesus], you love him; and even though you do not see him now, you believe in him and are filled with an inexpressible and glorious joy, for you are receiving the goal of faith, the salvation of your souls.

1 Peter 1:8–9

Jesus said, "Until now you have not asked for anything in my name. Ask and you will receive, and your joy will be complete."

John 16:24

Those who sow in tears will reap with songs of joy.

Psalm 126:5

You turned my wailing into dancing; you removed my sackcloth and clothed me with joy, that my heart may sing to you and not be silent. O Lord my God, I will give you thanks forever

Psalm 30:11-12

[God] will yet fill your mouth with laughter and your lips with shouts of joy.

Job 8:21

The Lord is my strength and my shield; my heart trusts in him, and I am helped. My heart leaps for joy, and I will give thanks to him in song.

Psalm 51:12

Restore to me the joy of your salvation and grant me a willing spirit, to sustain me.

Psalm 51:12

Let all who take refuge in you be glad, [O Lord]; let them ever sing for joy.

Psalm 5:11

You make me glad by your deeds, O Lord; I sing for joy at the words of your hands.

Psalm 92:4

The precepts of the Lord are right, giving joy to the heart.

Psalm 19:8

When anxiety was great within me, your consolation brought joy to my soul.

Psalm 94:19

Your statutes are my heritage forever, [O Lord]; they are the joy of my heart.

Psalm 119:111

The Lord declares, "You will go out in joy and be led forth in peace; the mountains and hills will burst into song before you, and all the trees of the field will clap their hands."

Isaiah 55:12

Shouts of joy and victory resound in the tents of the righteous: "The Lord's right hand has done mighty things!"

Psalm 118:15

The prospect of the righteous is joy.

Proverbs 10:28

Peace

I will lie down and sleep in peace, for you alone, O Lord, make me dwell in safety.

Psalm 4:8

The Lord gives strength to his people; The Lord blesses his people with peace.

Psalm 29:11

The meek will inherit the land and enjoy great peace.

Psalm 37:11

Consider the blameless, observe the upright; a future awaits those who seek peace.

Psalm 85:8

Love and faithfulness meet together; righteousness and peace kiss each other.

Psalm 85:10

Great peace have they who love your law, and nothing can make them stumble.

Psalm 119:165

Blessed are those who find wisdom, those who gain understanding . . . Her ways are pleasant ways, and all her paths are peace.

Proverbs 3: 13, 17

There is deceit in the hearts of those who plot evil, but joy for those who promote peace.

Proverbs 12:20

A heart at peace gives life to the body, but envy rots the bones.

Proverbs 14:30

Better a dry crust with peace and quiet than a house full of feasting, with strife.

Proverbs 17:1

Discipline your son, and he will give you peace; he will bring delight to your soul.

Proverbs 29:17

To us a child is born, to us a son is given . . . And he will be called . . . Prince of peace.

Isaiah 9:3

You will keep in perfect peace those whose minds are steadfast, because they trust in you.

Isaiah 26:3

When the Lord takes pleasure in anyone's way, he causes their enemies to make peace with them.

Proverbs 16:7

How beautiful on the mountains are the feet of those who bring good news, who proclaim peace.

Isaiah 52:7

He was pierced for our transgressions, He was crushed for our iniquities; the punishment that brought us peace was upon him, and by his wounds we are healed.

Isaiah 53:5

"Though the mountains be shaken and the hills be removed, yes my unfailing love for you will not be shaken, nor my covenant of peace be removed," says the Lord, who has compassion on you.

Isaiah 54:10

Those who walk uprightly enter into peace; they find rest as they lie in death.

Isaiah 57:2

Jesus said, "Peace I leave with you; my peace I give you. I do not give to you as the world gives. Do not let your hearts be troubled and do not be afraid."

John 14:27

Jesus said, "I have told you these things, so that in me you may have peace. In this world you will have trouble. But take heart! I have overcome the world."

John 16:33

Whatever is true, whatever is noble, whatever is right, whatever is pure, whatever is lovely, whatever is admirable—if anything is excellent or praiseworthy—think about such things. Whatever you have learned or received or heard from me, or seen in me—put it into practice. And the God of peace will be with you.

Philippians 4:8–9

All your children will be taught by the Lord, and great will be their peace.

Isaiah 54:13

[Christ] Himself is our peace.

Ephesians 2:14

Peacemakers who sow in peace raise a harvest of righteousness.

James 3:18

FAITHFULNESS

Jesus said, "His master replied, 'Well done, good and faithful servant! You have been faithful with a few things: I will put you in charge of many things. Come and share your master's happiness!"

Matthew 25:21

Be joyful in hope, patient in affliction, faithful in prayer.

Romans 12:12

It is required that those who have been given a trust must prove faithful.

1 Corinthians 4:2

The fruit of the Spirit is . . . faithfulness.

Galatians 5:22

I thank Christ Jesus our Lord, who has given me strength, that he considered me faithful, appointing me to his service.

1 Timothy 1:12

To the faithful you show yourself faithful.

Psalm 18:25

Each of you should use whatever gift you have received to serve others, as faithful stewards of God's grace in its various forms.

1 Peter 4:10

They will make war against the Lamb, but the Lamb will overcome them because he is Lord of lords and King of kings—and with him will be his called, chosen and faithful followers.

Revelation 17:14

Love the Lord, all His saints! The Lord preserves the faithful, but the proud He pays back in full.

Psalm 31:23

The Lord loves the just and will not forsake His faithful ones. They will be protected forever, but the offspring of the wicked will be cut off.

Psalm 37:28

Let those who love the Lord hate evil, for he guards the lives of his faithful ones and delivers them the hand of the wicked.

Psalm 97:10

My eyes will be on the faithful in the land, that they may dwell with me; Those whose walk is blameless will minister to me.

Psalm 101:6

The faithless will be fully repaid for their ways, and the good rewarded for theirs.

Proverbs 14:14

Many claim to have unfailing love, but a faithful person who can find?

Proverbs 20:6

Let love and faithfulness never leave you; Bind them around your neck, write them on the tablet of your heart. Then you will win favor and a good name in the sight of God and humankind.

Proverbs 3:3–4

Love and faithfulness keep a king safe; through love his throne is made secure.

Proverbs 20:28

A faithful person will be richly blessed, but one eager to get rich will not go unpunished.

Proverbs 28:20

Lazy hands make for poverty, but diligent hands bring wealth.

Proverbs 10:4

Diligent hands will rule, but laziness ends in slave labor.

Proverbs 12:24

The sluggard craves and gets nothing, but the desires of the diligent are fully satisfied.

Proverbs 13:4

The plans of the diligent lead to profit as surely as haste leads to poverty.

Proverbs 21:5

Don't let anyone look down on you because you are young, but set an example for the believers in speech, in life, in love, in faith and in purity . . . Devote yourself to the public reading of scripture, to preaching and to teaching. Do not neglect your gift . . . Be diligent in these matters; give yourself wholly to them, so that everyone may see your progress. Watch your life and doctrine closely. Persevere in them, because if you do, you will save both yourself and your hearers.

1 Timothy 4:12–16

Those who work their land will have abundant food, but those who chase fantasies have no sense.

Proverbs 12:11

All hard work brings a profit; their hunger drives them on.

Proverbs 14:23

A wife of noble character . . . works with eager hands. She sets about her work vigorously; her arms are strong for her tasks. She sees that her trading is profitable, and her lamp does not go out at night. Give her the reward she has earned, and let her works bring her praise at the city gate.

Proverbs 31:10, 13, 17–18, 31

Patience

Be joyful in hope, patient in affliction, faithful in prayer.

Romans 12:12

The end of a matter is better than its beginning, and patience is better than pride.

Ecclesiastes 7:8

If we hope for what we do not yet have, we wait for it patiently.

Romans 8:25

Be patient, then . . . until the Lord's coming. See how the farmer waits for the land to yield its valuable crop and how patient he is for the autumn and spring rains. You too, be patient and stand firm, because the Lord's coming is near.

James 5:7–8

We pray this in order that you may live a life worthy of the Lord and may please Him in every way: bearing fruit in every good work, growing in the knowledge of God, being strengthened with all power according to his glorious might so that you may have great endurance and patience.

Colossians 1:10–11

Through patience a ruler can be persuaded, and a gentle tongue can break a bone.

Proverbs 25:15

Those who are patient have great understanding, but the quick-tempered display folly.

Proverbs 14:29

The Lord is not slow in keeping his promise, as some understand slowness. He is patient with you, not waiting anyone to perish, but everyone to come to repentance.

2 Peter 3:9

A person's wisdom yields patience; it is to one's glory to overlook an offense.

Proverbs 19:11

As God's chosen people, holy and dearly loved, clothe yourselves with compassion, kindness, humility, gentleness, and patience.

Colossians 3:12

Preach the Word; be prepared in season and out of season, correct, rebuke and encourage—with great patience and careful instruction.

2 Timothy 4:2

We do not want you to become lazy, but to imitate those who through faith and patience inherit what has been promised.

Hebrews 6:12

A hot-tempered man stirs up dissension, but a patient man calms a quarrel.

Proverbs 15:18

Watch your life and doctrine closely. Persevere in them, because if you do, you will save both yourself and your hearers.

1 Timothy 4:16

Do not throw away your confidence; it will be richly rewarded. You need to persevere so that when you have done the will of God, you will receive what he has promised.

Hebrews 10:35–36

Blessed are those who persevere under trial, because when they have stood the test, they will receive the crown of life that God has promised to those who love him.

James 1:12

We . . . rejoice in our sufferings, because we know that suffering produces perseverance; perseverance, character; and character, hope.

Romans 5:3–4

The testing of your faith produces perseverance. Let perseverance finish its work so that you may be mature and complete, not lacking anything.

James 1:3–4

We consider blessed those who have persevered. You have heard of Job's perseverance and have seen what the Lord finally brought about. The Lord is full of compassion and mercy.

James 5:11

Let us not become weary in doing good, for at the proper time we will reap a harvest if we do not give up.

Galatians 6:9

The Lord of all grace, who called you to his eternal glory in Christ, after you have suffered a little while, will himself restore you and make you strong, firm and steadfast.

1 Peter 5:10

Jesus said, "He who stands firm to the end will be saved."

Matthew 10:22

Truthful lips endure forever, but a lying tongue lasts only a moment.

Proverbs 12:19

When we are cursed, we bless; when we are persecuted, we endure it; when we are slandered, we answer kindly.

1 Corinthians 4:12–13

Be strong in the grace that is in Christ Jesus . . . Endure hardship with us like a good soldier of Christ Jesus.

2 Timothy 2:1, 3

Not that I have already obtained all this, or have already been made perfect, but I press on to take hold of that for which Christ Jesus took hold of me . . . I do not consider myself yet to have taken hold of it. But one thing I do: Forgetting what is behind and straining toward what is ahead, I press on toward the goal to win the prize for which God has called me heavenward in Christ Jesus.

Philippians 3:12–14

Here is a trustworthy saying: If we died with Him, we will also live with Him; if we endure, we will also reign with Him.

2 Timothy 2:11–12

Let us not become weary in doing good, for at the proper time we will reap a harvest if we do not give up.

Galatians 6:9

Jesus told His disciples a parable to show them that they should always pray and not give up.

Luke 18:1

FRIENDSHIP

Making a thousand friends a year is not a miracle. The miracle is to make a friend who stands by you for a thousand years.

* * *

A friend is one who knows who you are, understands where you have been, accepts what you have become, and still gently allows you to grow.

* * *

Good friends are hard to find, harder to leave, and impossible to forget.

* * *

You were there in the beginning, and I know you'll wait in the end, but most importantly, in between you've been my best friend.

* * *

When it hurts to look back and you are scared to look ahead, look beside you and your best friend will be there.

* * *

A true friend will always be there when the whole world leaves you; he always cheers you up when the whole world turns you down, and he never asks you to act like an angel but becomes your angel.

* * *

I've been searching for that someone, to show me the way; I've been searching for that someone, and now I know it's true, I've found that special one, I've found that someone in you.

* * *

Me and you are friends . . . you fight, I fight . . . you hurt, I hurt . . . you cry, I cry . . . you jump off a bridge . . . I'm gonna miss you forever.

* * *

Thank you for the friendship you have offered; rest assured that I'll treasure it in my heart and will always remember that once in my life, I've known someone like you.

* * *

As I look on my past, I remember the jokes I laughed at, the things I missed and lost, but there's one thing I'll never regret: it's the day you became my friend.

* * *

I will always be there for you, through the good times and the bad, the smooth and the rough, or just any other time you need somebody . . . just look for me, and I will be there for you.

* * *

Friends should be the ones listening to your secrets, not the ones that hurt your feelings without knowing. Friends should be ones that keep all your secrets, not those who spread it all around.

* * *

A great friend is someone who makes your problems their problems just so you don't have to go through them alone.

* * *

A true friend walks in when the whole world walks out.

* * *

A friend is someone who accepts your past, supports your present, and encourages your future.

* * *

Finding a true friend is like panning for gold. You have to sift through the fakes to find the real ones.

LOVE

Spread love everywhere you go: first of all in your own house. Give love to your children, to your wife or husband, to a next door neighbor . . . Let no one ever come to you without leaving better and happier. Be the living expression of God's kindness; kindness in your face, kindness in your eyes, kindness in your smile, kindness in your warm greeting.

* * *

Love consists in desiring to give what is our own to another and feeling his delight as our own.

* * *

If you love someone you would be willing to give up everything for them, but if they loved back they'd never ask you to.

* * *

When it comes down to love, you risk nothing or everything. That's just how it is.

* * *

There is always something left to love, and if you ain't learned that, you ain't learned nothing.

* * *

Love is a circle that doth restless move in the same sweet eternity of love.

* * *

Love is when you don't want to go to sleep, because reality is better than a dream.

* * *

The magic words for a great relationship are "I love you just the way you are."

* * *

Love works a different way in different minds; the fool it enlightens and the wise it blinds.

* * *

Love is like a mustard seed, planted by God and watered by men.

* * *

Love, like a river, will cut a new path whenever it meets an obstacle.

* * *

Love is a puzzle posed by emotions and not likely to be solved by reason.

* * *

Love is not sweet talks and flowers, but love is forgiving and compromising.

* * *

True love is not the number of kisses, or how often you get them; true love is the feeling that still lingers long after the kiss is over.

* * *

Love that does not show love is not love. It is illusion.

* * *

Love consists in desiring to give what is our own to another and feeling his delight as our own.

* * *

Love can never be taught, for it is to be learned; love can never be bought, for it is to be given; love can never be old, for it lives to last a lifetime.

* * *

Love is like swallowing hot chocolate before it has cooled off. It takes you by surprise at first but keeps you warm for a long time.

* * *

You can't make someone love you. All you can do is be someone who can be loved. The rest is up to the person to realize your worth.

* * *

Love is a VERB . . . an action we CHOOSE to carry out. Take action today and show the ones you love how you feel about them.

* * *

Love is what makes you smile when you're tired.

* * *

Love expects no reward. Love knows no fear. Love Divine gives—does not demand. Love thinks no evil, imputes no motive. To love is to share and serve.

* * *

I tell you I love every day for fear that tomorrow isn't another.

* * *

Love is sweet when it's new, but sweeter when it's true.

* * *

Love is what is left in a relationship after all the selfishness has been removed.

* * *

Love has no desire but to fulfill itself. To melt and be like a running brook that sings its melody to the night. To wake at dawn with a winged heart and give thanks for another day of loving.

* * *

As you melt this heart of stone you take my hand to guide me home and now I'm in love.

* * *

You may never know how important you are to me or how much I care for you, but you are and you will always be. Bear in mind that I couldn't afford to lose someone I've learned to care about so much.

* * *

Do you love me because I am beautiful or am I beautiful because you love me?

* * *

True love brings up everything you're allowing a mirror to be held up to you daily.

* * *

There is only one thing that can never die: LOVE.

* * *

To love another person is to see the face of God.

* * *

Love distills desire in the eyes; love brings bewitching grace into the heart.

* * *

Love is the basic need of human nature, for without it life is disrupted emotionally, mentally, spiritually, and physically.

* * *

Everyone admits that love is wonderful and necessary, yet no one agrees on just what it is.

* * *

When we first fall in love, we feel that we know all there is to know about life, and perhaps we are right.

* * *

Take love, multiply it by infinite, and take it to the depth of forever . . . And you still have only a glimpse of how I feel for you.

* * *

Perhaps love is the process of my gently leading you back to yourself.

* * *

A happy marriage has in it all the pleasures of friendships, all the enjoyment of sense and reason—and indeed all the sweets of life.

* * *

A man falls in love through his eyes, a woman through her ears.

* * *

Love is that condition in which the happiness of another person is essential to your own.

* * *

Love in its essence is spiritual fire.

* * *

Love can kneel in front of you as a blessing, as it can never end.

* * *

Love is the only sane and satisfying answer to the problem of human existence.

* * *

Love is a quality, not a quantity.

* * *

Love is smiling on the inside and out.

* * *

The essence of romantic love is that wonderful beginning, after which sadness and impossibility may become the rule.

* * *

Love is the big booming beat that covers up the noise of hate.

* * *

Love is the enchanted dawn of every heart.

* * *

True love stories never have endings.

* * *

True love is a wonder that has no end or beginning.

* * *

Love does not dominate; it cultivates.

* * *

Love is the essence of God.

* * *

Love is content with the present, it hopes for the future, and it doesn't brood over the past.

* * *

Love is not what we become, but who we already are.

* * *

In the arithmetic of love, one plus one equals everything, and two minus one equals nothing.

* * *

Love is the strongest force the world possesses, and yet it is the humblest imaginable.

* * *

Suddenly the world seems such a perfect place; suddenly it moves with such a perfect grace. Suddenly my life doesn't seem such a waste; it all revolves around you.

* * *

Love builds bridges where there are none.

* * *

To get the full value of a joy you must have somebody to divide with.

* * *

Love is like a pen; you can try to scratch it off but can't erase it.

* * *

Darkness cannot drive out darkness. Only light can do that. Hate cannot drive out hate; only love can do that.

* * *

Love me now, love me never, but if you love me, love me forever.

* * *

Love not only forgives but it also seeks forgiveness.

* * *

Love is like a baby; it needs to be treated gently.

* * *

In doing something, do it with love or never do it at all.

* * *

Love is not finding someone to live with; it's finding someone you can't live without.

* * *

Love cures people—both the ones who give it and the ones who receive it.

* * *

At the touch of love, everyone is a poet.

* * *

Where there is love there is life.

* * *

Once you love, you can't undo it. What you felt may have changed, shifted slightly, yet still remains love.

* * *

Where there is love, there is no imposition.

* * *

Love is like violin. The music may stop now and then, but the strings remain forever.

* * *

Love is an ideal thing, marriage is a real thing.

* * *

Love is a many-splendored thing. Love lifts us up where we belong. All you need is love.

BIBLIOGRAPHY

CHAPTER 1

1. See Galatians 5:22–23.
2. See John 3:16.
3. See Daniel 1:8.
4. See Esther 2:17.

CHAPTER 2

1. Preventing poor decisions can be a significant way to avoid later problems.
2. One of the best discussions of true friendship that I have read is a chapter titled, "The Ideals of Spiritual Friendship," in David G. Benner, *Sacred Companions: The Gift of Spiritual Friendship and Direction* (Downers Grove, IL: InterVarsity, 2002), 61–84.
3. See Romans 12:16–18.
4. See Proverbs 13:20.
5. See 1 Thessalonians 5:11.
6. See Galatians 5:13–15.

CHAPTER 3

1. See 1 Peter 1:22.
2. See 1 Peter 3:8–9.
3. See Colossians 3:13–16.

CHAPTER 5

1. See 1 Corinthians 13:–8
2. See James 2:8.
3. See Ephesians 3:17–19.

4. See Song of Songs 8:7.
5. See Song of Songs 7:10.
6. See Colossians 4:6.
7. See Titus 2:7–8.

Chapter 7

1. See Genesis 2:18.
2. See Matthew 19:11–12.
3. See 1 Corinthians 7:7.
4. See 1 Corinthians 7:28, 32–35.
5. Researcher George Barna makes this point in *Single Focus* (Ventura, CA: Regal Books, 2003). Too often, discussions about singles lump all unmarried people together, overlooking the significant diversity within the singles population.
6. This is from the 2000 US Census as reported by Feinberg in "Single and Fabulous."
7. According to Lauren F. Winner, "Three surveys of single Christians conducted in the 1990s turned up a lot of premarital sex. Approximately one-third of the respondents were virgins—that means, of course, that two-thirds not." Lauren F. Winner, "Sex in the Body of Christ," *Christianity Today* 49 (May 2005): 28–33.
8. See 1 Corinthians 7:9.

Chapter 8

1. An Internet search will reveal a number of books devoted to single parenting. These include Gary Richmond, *Successful Single Parenting* (Eugene, OR: Harvest House, 1998); Armin A. Brott, *The Single Father: A Dad's Guide to Parenting without a Partner* (New York: Abbeville Press, 1999); and Michelle Howe, *Going It Alone: Meeting the Challenge of Being a Single Mom* (Peabody, MA: Hendrickson,1999).
2. Lauren F. Winner, "The Four Pillars of Wisdom: Helping Singles Counteract Conflicting Cultural Messages," *Psychotherapy Networker* 24 (2000): 75.
3. Winner, "Sex in the Body of Christ," 30

4. Sharon Morris, "Singles, Sex, and Celibacy," *Christian Counseling Today* 9 (2001): 47–49.

CHAPTER 9

1. This is the title of a popular book written by twenty-one-year-old Joshua Harris. With its emphasis on viewing love, purity, and singleness from God's perspective rather than thinking that love and romance are to be enjoyed "solely for recreation," this book "turned the Christian singles scene upside down," according to one reviewer, and at the time of this writing, sales were approaching one million copies. Joshua Harris, *I Kissed Dating Goodbye*, updated edition (Sisters, OR: Multinomah, 2003).
2. See Hebrews 12:15–16.

CHAPTER 11

1. See Genesis 6:11, 13.
2. See Luke 22:24.
3. See Acts 5, 6:1, 15:2, 7.
4. See Acts 15:36–41 and Galatians 2:11–21.
5. 2 Corinthians 12:20–21.
6. See Proverbs 10:18–19; 12:22; 15:1, 28, 31; 16:24, 28; 17:9; 19:22; 24:26; 26:20; and 28:23.

CHAPTER 12

1. For more information about how affairs happen, the various types of affairs, and how to find healing, see Joe Beam, *Becoming One* (West Monroe, LA: Howard Publishing, 1999).
2. See also Drs. Hatley and Chalmers, *Surviving an Affair* (Old Tappan, NJ: Fleming Revell Company, 1998).
3. See 1 Timothy 5:16.
4. See 1 Timothy 5:8.
5. See Matthew 16:26.
6. See Ephesians 4:25.
7. See Exodus 13 and Deuteronomy 6 for the basis for the tradition.

CHAPTER 14

1. See 1 Corinthians 7.
2. See Romans 13:14 and 1 Corinthians 7:9.
3. See, for example, Exodus 20:14, 17 and Matthew 5:32.
4. See Exodus 22:16–19, Leviticus 18:20, Deuteronomy 5:18 and 22:23–34, Matthew 5:27–30, and John 8:4.
5. See 1 Corinthians 6:13, 18.
6. See Isaiah 57:3, Jeremiah 3:8–9, Ezekiel 23:43, James 4:4, and Revelation 2:20, 23.
7. See Exodus 20:14, Leviticus 18:20, Deuteronomy 5:18 and 22:23–34, Matthew 5:27–30, and John 8:4.
8. See 1 Corinthians 7:9.
9. See Genesis 1:27–28, 31.
10. See Genesis 2:25 and 3:9–11.
11. For a discussion of masturbation published in a magazine for young Christians, see Dave Roberts, "U Can't Touch That: What Does the Bible Really Say about Masturbation," *Relevant* 7 (2004): 52–53.
12. Some have argued that the sin of Onan, described in Genesis 38, is a form of masturbation because he spilled his semen on the ground. Even a casual reading of the text indicates, however, that Onan's sin involved disobedience to God by refusing to impregnate the wife of his deceased brother, as Old Testament law required.
13. See Philippians 4:8 and 1 Corinthians 10:31.
14. See 1 Corinthians 6:12.

CHAPTER 17

1. See 1 Kings 1:5, 6.
2. See 1 Samuel 2.
3. It should be noted, however, that many of the biblical passages that we have cited in this section appear to focus less on family dynamics and more on the ways in which God works through key men and women.
4. See Colossians 3:18–21.
5. See Ephesians 5:22–6:4. Ephesians has 16 of 155 verses devoted to the family.

6. In 1 Thessalonians 2:7–12, Paul gives an illustration from the home. 1 Timothy mentions the care of widows and makes a statement about Timothy's home. In Titus, there is an exhortation to wives and mothers.
7. See Ephesians 5:25.
8. See Ephesians 6:4. Proverbs 22:6 is one of several Old Testament verses on child-rearing.
9. This is the first of a list of family traits that was developed from a survey by an author who was quoted widely a few years ago. See Dolores Curran, *Traits of a Healthy Family* (Minneapolis: Winston Press, 1983). Other traits on the list include these: develop a sense of play and humor, share responsibility, have a sense of right and wrong, have a strong sense of family in which rituals and traditions abound, and admit and seek help with problems.
10. See 1 Timothy 5:8.
11. See Esther 4:14.
12. See Esther 8:6.
13. See K. W. Simon, "Fatherhood in the Middle Years," (Master's thesis, University of Nebraska, Lincoln, 1982).
14. See Malachi 2:13–16.
15. See Matthew 19:8.
16. See Ephesians 5:25.
17. See Ephesians 5:28.
18. See Titus 2:4.
19. Other prominent scholars across the country have models of normal families or healthy families with eight, twelve, or fifteen qualities included. These models and this research are also in agreement. The issue is not how many qualities it takes to define a strong family. The important thing to keep in mind is that there is remarkable agreement among researchers and scholars regarding the general outline of what constitutes a strong family. If you'd like to read more about the other research mentioned here, see M. Kyrysan, K. A. Moore, and N. Zill, *Identifying Successful Families: An Overview of Constructs and Selected Measures* (Washington, DC: Child Trends, 1990).

Chapter 20

1. A recent national survey stated that 79 percent of the 2,013 adults surveyed in January 2002 by the research group Public Agenda said a lack of respect and courtesy in American society is a serious problem. Many people feel awkward and insecure in meeting people or introducing them to others in a social setting. This chapter covers essential basics to help the family feel good about themselves.
2. Sadly, morals, manners, and spiritual values have declined. The Golden Rule, "Do to others as you would have them to do you" (Luke 6:31), which is of every major religion, expresses the key to manners and how we should act in life in the family.

About the Author

Denise P. Lafortune, characterized by dynamic prayer, powerful worship, and relevant preaching of the Word, has encouraged and transformed a lot of hearts. She hosts radio programs and often shares her insights in women's ministries. In addition, she is passionate about youths and has a tremendous vision to see them excel and build a healthier youth ministry. She is the president/founder of International Federation of Youth Conquerors, Inc. Denise has a master's degree in Arts of Counseling and Doctorate in Ministry. She speaks locally, nationally, and internationally about bringing back the glory to the house of the Lord.